Flirt skirts

To those of you looking to make your passion your livelihood,
we dedicate this book to you.

A QUIRK PACKAGING BOOK

Copyright © 2011 by Quirk Packaging, Inc.

All rights reserved.

Published in the United States by Potter Craft,
an imprint of the Crown Publishing Group,
a division of Random House, Inc., New York.
www.crownpublishing.com
www.pottercraft.com
POTTER CRAFT and colophon is a registered trademark of Random House, Inc.

Library of Congress Cataloging-in-Publication Data is available upon request.

ISBN: 978-0-307-58669-8

Printed in China

Edited by Erin Canning
Art direction by Lynne Yeamans
Design and illustrations by woolypear
Photography © Barbara Sullivan
Additional photography © Mark A. Gore: pp. 23, 25, 41, 43, 45, 53, 55, 58, 61, 64, 79, 81, 99

10 9 8 7 6 5 4 3 2 1

First Edition

Flirt skirts

LEARN HOW TO *sew*, *customize*, AND *style* YOUR VERY OWN SKIRTS

PATTI GILSTRAP
& SERYN POTTER

Photography by Barbara Sullivan

POTTER
CRAFT

Contents

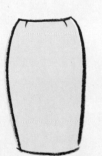

Introduction

After owning boutiques and designing and making clothes for more than ten years, we've come to realize a basic truth about clothing: It's not about fabric, although a beautiful fabric can certainly transform a simple piece. It's not about trends, although some trends can be just right for your shape. It's about fit; a good fit is the hardest thing to attain because off-the-rack clothing is made to a certain set of standards that often don't work with *our* body shapes.

As part of our quest to help our customers find the fit they were looking for, we started a custom-skirt service at our shop. With seven different skirt styles and hundreds of fabrics to choose from, we let our customers "design" their own skirts, putting the creativity into their hands. After trying on our basic-skirt samples, they determine the alterations to be made—shorter, longer, high-waisted, low-sitting, etc. Based on customer feedback and what we've seen firsthand as being the most desirable and best-fitting across the range of body types, the A-line, Pencil, and Flare skirts are our most tried-and-true styles. We have tweaked these skirts through the years, and the result is three extremely flattering silhouettes that we are sharing with you. Once you master sewing these basic-skirt shapes, the possibilities will be truly endless when it comes to making something flattering to wear. And because these shapes are basic, they will act as a blank canvas for your creativity.

Using this book is simple. After introducing you to the sewing basics, we discuss the fit of the three basic-skirt styles; then we show you how to work with the patterns and templates. When you reach the Building Your Basic Skirt section, regard this section as something of a skirt-making bible since the basic skirts are the foundations for each project. The Pin-fitting step is extremely important, especially if you want to obtain the perfect fit for your body. Then we show you twenty techniques, including appliquéing, pleating, printing, and design stitching, to transform your basic skirts into unique and exciting garments. You'll be amazed at how these techniques enhance the basic skirts. You can also try out these techniques on all of the basic-skirt styles, not just the one that is demonstrated in the book. As you progress through the book and the projects, your mastery of these skills will improve and hopefully inspire you to come up with your own variations.

As you become more familiar with our fit and design techniques, you will discover what works best for you, which will not only improve your sewing skills but also make you a better shopper. You will begin to look for certain elements that you may not have thought to notice before. We hope, in the end, *Flirt Skirts* will help you create a closet full of clothes that are not only exciting to wear but well-fitting, too!

Happy sewing!

—Patti Gilstrap and Seryn Potter

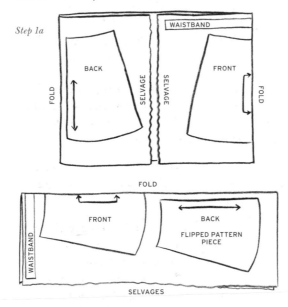

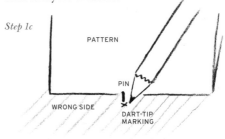

Altering

If your waist size is sm
follow these instructio
your skirt style.

A-line

1. Measure your side
from your natural wai
your hips.

2. Measure down the
piece this distance; th
add ⅜" (10mm) for th
a mark on your side se

EXAMPLE: If your wa
10" (25cm): 10" (25c
= 6⅜" (16cm).

3. For every size your
waist size, add ½" (13
beyond your side-sea

EXAMPLE: If your wa
a size 8, make a mark
seam.

4. Starting from the c
depending on which
on, draw a horizontal
this mark, for your ne

5. Connect the waist-
like the curve on the
hip line to the hem, c

6. Repeat Steps 2–5

1. Lay Out the Pattern and Cut Your Fabric

a. Fold your fabric in half selvage to selvage, right sides together. Fold it one of two ways, depending on the width of your fabric:

Step 1a

The skirt-front and waistband (Flare skirt only) patterns are placed on the fold of the fabric; the skirt-back pattern is laid out on two layers of fabric, so that the pattern's grain line is parallel to your fabric's selvage edge.

NOTE: To double-check that your pattern's grain line is parallel to your fabric's selvage edge, measure from the selvage to the grain line at the top, middle, and bottom of your grain line to make sure all measurements are the same.

b. Once your pattern pieces are laid out, pin them to the fabric. Cut out the fabric, making sure to cut the notches marked on the pattern away from your cutting line, leaving a mirror image on the cut-fabric edge.

c. Before unpinning the pattern, transfer the dart markings to your fabric by snipping (making very small cuts) into the fabric in line with the dart legs (the lines that form the dart). To transfer the dart tip (the point of the dart) from pattern to fabric, stick a pin through the dart tip, going through the pattern and both fabric layers. Pull back the paper to expose the spot where the pin pierces the fabric; at that puncture point, make a small mark with tailor's chalk on the wrong sides of both layers of fabric.

Step 1c

TIP: *If you are working with a fabric that looks similar on both sides, mark the wrong side with a piece of tape now, so you don't get confused later.*

d. Unpin the pattern from your fabric.

2. Stay-Stitch Your Waistband

Before unfolding your skirt front, place a pin at the center top (to remind yourself where the center is), then unfold it. Stay-stitch (a straight stitch sewn to prevent curves from stretching out) ⅜" (10mm) from the top-cut edge: start at the left edge and sew to the center, stop, flip over your skirt front, and stay-stitch from the non-sewn edge to the center. Repeat on both skirt-back pieces, remembering to sew from the side of each piece to the center.

3. Sew Your Invisible Zipper and Center-Back Seam

a. Use an over-edge zigzag stitch to finish the center-back seam edges on your skirt-back pieces.

b. On the wrong side of the zipper, make three marks on the tape on either side of the teeth; these markings will guide you in sewing in a flat zipper. The top mark should be about ⅝" (16mm) from the top of the zipper; the next mark should be 4" (10cm) from the first mark; and the last mark should be 4" (10cm) from the second mark.

c. Lay the zipper wrong side up on the right side of the left-back skirt piece. The stopper of the zipper should be ⅜" (10mm) from the top-cut edge. With tailor's chalk, make three marks on the fabric that correspond to the markings on the zipper tape.

d. Unzip the zipper and pin the right zipper tape to the right side of the left-back skirt piece so that the zipper teeth are ⅝" (16mm) from the finished-seam edge. Using your sewing machine's invisible zipper foot, sew ⅝" (16mm) from the finished-seam edge, making sure the chalk marks on the zipper and fabric stay aligned as you sew. When you reach the bottom of the zipper, sew as far as the zipper foot will allow.

e. Lay the right-back piece right side up next to the left-back piece that has the zipper sewn in. Transfer the three corresponding chalk marks on the left-back piece to the right-back piece.

f. Match the zipper markings to the fabric markings, this time, pinning the left zipper tape to the right side of the right-back skirt piece.

g. Face the right sides of the two skirt-back pieces together and close the zipper. Pin the rest of the center-back seam together below the zipper. Using the zipper foot, start sewing approximately two stitches below where you stopped sewing the zipper, making sure you don't catch the bottom of the zipper in the seam. Sew a ⅝" (16mm) seam allowance.

h. Press the seam allowance open, turn the skirt right side out, and press over the zipper. The invisible zipper should look like it's part of the seam.

> **TIP:** *If you see a lot of zipper tape, your stitches are not as close to the teeth as they should be. Not a problem! Open the zipper and stitch a bit closer to the teeth. There's no need to remove the other stitches; they'll be hidden in your seam allowance.*

i. On the wrong side of your skirt back, tack down the bottommost edge of the zipper tape to the seam allowance only. Just a few stitches done with the zipper foot will keep the bottom edge of the zipper from flipping to the right side of the garment.

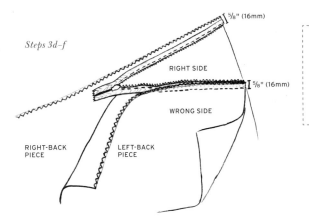

Steps 3d–f

⅝" (16mm)

RIGHT SIDE

⅝" (16mm)

WRONG SIDE

RIGHT-BACK PIECE   LEFT-BACK PIECE

4. Pin-Fit Your Skirt

Before going any further, it is time to see how the skirt pieces are coming together on *you*. Every person has a different set of waist *and* hip measurements and waist-*to*-hip measurements, as well as a preference for where she likes her skirt to sit—be it on the natural waist, hips, or in-between. Pin-fitting makes these adjustments easier. When pin-fitting, we prefer to use safety pins instead of straight pins, because straight pins can wiggle out of your fabric, losing your fit information. Now that we've told you the why of the pin-fit, let's get into the how.

a. Match up your skirt front and back, right sides together. A ⅝" (16mm) seam allowance is allotted for your side seams, so place safety pins at this distance. Now is when your seam gauge really comes in handy: set the gauge to ⅝" (16mm) and use it as a guide, placing a safety pin every 3" (7.5 cm). Do this for both the right- and left-side seams.

Step 4a

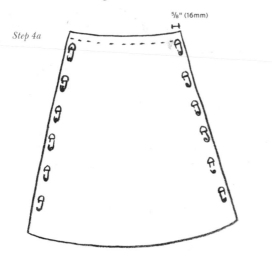

⅝" (16mm)

b. Pin the darts closed (two darts for A-line; four darts for Pencil). Match up the cuts you made earlier in the fabric edge (Step 1c, page 16) and pinch the fabric right sides together. Stick a safety pin in, piercing through both layers of fabric. Repeat for all darts.

NOTE: If you forget this step, your skirt will be too big. The darts are integrated into the pattern for shaping purposes.

c. Put your skirt on inside out with the pins visible to you and close the zipper. Stand in front of a mirror, so you can see how things are going. Any adjustments you make should be symmetrical between the right- and left-side seams.

EXAMPLE: If your skirt is 2" (5cm) too big, evenly distribute the amount of fabric you're going to take in by pinching 1" (2.5cm) from the left seam and 1" (2.5cm) from the right seam.

d. Put your skirt on right side out, hiding the pins and seam allowances, to get a more realistic look. Take into consideration that your skirt has hem and waist allowances, so it isn't the exact length of the finished skirt just yet—but it's close enough to give you an idea of the fit.

Things You Should Think About While Pin-Fitting Your Skirt

1. **Do I like where the top of the skirt sits on my body?** You have a ³⁄₈" (10mm) seam allowance at the top of the skirt, so keep this in mind when making adjustments. If you would like the skirt to sit higher on your waistline, move the pins in from the cut edges to make your skirt smaller. If you would like the skirt to sit lower on your hips, move the pins out toward the cut edges so that the skirt is bigger. If you would like to add more curve to the back of your skirt, pinch more fabric into the darts, making sure to move your pins as evenly as possible.

2. **Do the curves on the seam match the curves of my body?** Some women are straighter from waist to hips, while others are much curvier. Adjust your pins so that they reflect your body shape, remembering to move both sets of pins equidistantly to create balance.

3. **Does my fabric have enough stretch to eliminate some of the ease?** Ease is the number of inches (centimeters) beyond your body measurements that are integrated into a pattern to allow you the capacity to move and bend freely. These days, many fabrics have a good amount of stretch to them, which allows you to make tighter-fitting garments that are also comfortable.

4. **What are my fit preferences?** Some people like their clothes to be tight-fitting, while others prefer things to be a bit looser. We like our A-lines low, our Pencils high, and our Flares somewhere in between. If you are unsure about your fit preferences, think about your favorite skirts and why you love them.

5. Sew Your Side Seams

a. If you did not make any changes when pin-fitting, stitch the side seams at ⁵⁄₈" (16mm) seam allowance; if you adjusted the pins, chalk a vertical mark over each safety pin, remove the pins, then connect your vertical marks into a continuous line on both sides of your skirt. Sew along these new stitching lines.

b. If you stitched the side seams at ⁵⁄₈" (16mm) seam allowance, finish the seam allowances; if you adjusted the pins, first trim the side-seam allowances to ⁵⁄₈" (16mm), then finish them.

> **TIP:** *You have two options for finishing your side seams: you can sew the two edges together with an over-edge zigzag stitch and press toward the back of your skirt; or you can sew each edge separately with an over-edge zigzag stitch and press the seam open flat (as is typically done for the center-back seam). We recommend sewing thinner fabrics together and thicker fabrics separately.*

6. Sew Your Darts

If you're sewing a Flare skirt, you can skip this section and move on to Sew Your Waistband (Step 7, page 20).

a. If you did not change the darts during your pin-fitting, follow the markings you transferred to the fabric in Step 1c. If you adjusted the darts, chalk a new stitching line for each one.

b. Starting with the first dart, match up the cuts for the dart legs, one on top of the other, with the right sides of the fabric together, creating a fold. Keep the fold on your right and the main part of the skirt on your left. Slide the two layers over each other until the chalk mark that represents the dart tip is on the fold. Securely pin the dart down. Repeat for the rest of the darts.

c. Take a piece of basting or masking tape that's slightly longer than the length of the dart, and lay it down so that the right edge of the tape makes a straight line from the cut marks to the mark at the tip of the dart.

Step 6c

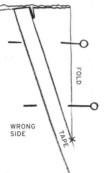

d. Sew right next to the tape (not on it). Start at the top of the dart where the cuts are, lockstitch, sew along the right side of the tape, then lockstitch again when you reach the dart tip.

TIP: *If you are working with a very thin or stretchy fabric, forgo lockstitching at the dart tip. Instead, change the stitch length to the smallest stitch on your machine and sew the last 1" (2.5cm) in this tighter stitch, continuing right off the fabric and leaving 1" (2.5cm) of thread hanging off. This gives the dart a nice flat bottom.*

NOTE: Make sure your paired darts are the same length; the back darts should be the same length, as should the front darts. Adjust, if necessary, before pressing them into place.

e. Place your skirt inside out on the ironing board and press each pair of darts toward the center of your skirt.

TIP: *Press only the dart fabric so that the dart blends in with the rest of the skirt fabric. Always check the dart from the outside of the garment to make sure you don't have any puckering.*

7. Sew Your Waistband

Now that your skirt fits well, it's time to add the waistband. If you are making an A-line or Pencil skirt, follow the instructions below; if you are making a Flare skirt, follow the instructions on page 22.

A-line and Pencil Skirts

a. Measure the circumference of the top of your skirt and add 1¼" (3cm) for a seam allowance. Cut a piece of bias tape to the same length.

TIP: *Get creative with the color of the bias tape for your waistband. Though it will not be seen from the outside of your skirt, a little pop of contrasting color is always a nice detail.*

b. Pin the bias tape right side up to the top of your skirt on the right side of the fabric, starting at the zipper: Open the zipper and extend the bias tape ⅝" (16mm) over the zipper edge. As you make your way around the skirt, cover the stay-stitching and also slightly overlap the top-cut edge with the bias tape, until the tape extends ⅝" (16mm) past the other side of the zipper. Do a "zipper check": close the zipper and make sure both pieces of bias tape are pinned in the same position on the skirt—one should not be higher than the other. Adjust the placement, if necessary.

c. Sew closely to the bias tape's lower edge. Trim any threads and/or fabric extending past the bias tape no thinner than $3/8$" (10mm)—you don't want to compromise the seam.

d. Fold the ends of the bias tape toward the wrong side of the fabric; then fold the rest of the bias tape toward the wrong side of your skirt, far enough over so that you cannot see it from the outside. Pin the tape in place all around your skirt. Do another zipper check to make sure that both sides of the skirt are even with each other.

Step 7d

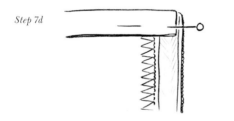

> **TIP:** *When pinning, place the pinheads to the right; doing this will make it easier for you to pull them out while sewing.*

e. Sew closely to the bias tape's lower edge; this stitching line will be visible, so try to keep your stitches straight. Start and stop your stitches about $1/4$" (6mm) from the teeth, so there is enough space for the zipper pull to make it all the way to the top of your skirt.

f. Place your skirt inside out on the ironing board, and press the entire top of the skirt to flatten it out and give it a nice, crisp edge.

Flare Skirt

g. Use an iron to fuse the interfacing, shiny side down, to the wrong side of the waistband piece.

h. Start pinning the waistband to the top of your skirt where the right back meets the zipper: Open the zipper and overlap your waistband $5/8$" (16mm) past the zipper edge, with the top edge of the waistband even with the top-cut edge of the skirt, right sides together. Pin both layers together until you reach the other side of the zipper.

NOTE: There may be anywhere from $1^7/8$" (4.5cm) up to 5" (12.5cm) of extra waistband fabric, depending on if you made adjustments during your pin-fit.

i. Do not trim off the excess fabric yet. Do a zipper check, closing the zipper to make sure the top comes together evenly. Sew a $5/8$" (16mm) seam allowance all the way around the top of your skirt to attach the waistband. Trim the left edge of the waistband down to $1^7/8$" (4.5cm); if you made no adjustments, it should already be this length.

j. Fold your waistband in half, right sides together. On the right-back side, sew the edge of the waistband at a $5/8$" (16mm) seam allowance, stopping $5/8$" (16mm) from the bottom corner. On the left-back side, sew the edge at a $5/8$" (16mm) seam allowance, pivot $5/8$" (16mm) from the bottom corner, then continue sewing $1^1/4$" (3cm).

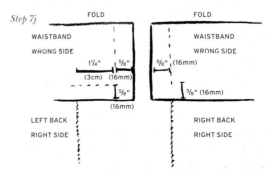

Step 7j

k. Clip the excess fabric from the corners and press the seam allowance up toward the waistband. Turn the waistband right side out. Poke out the corners of the button tabs (the extended fabric on the left-back side of the waistband where the buttonhole will be made and the fabric edge opposite where the button will be placed) with your point turner.

l. Fold the unattached waistband edge under $^3/_8$" (10mm) on the inside of the skirt, so that the fold hangs a bit lower than the seam you stitched in Step 7i. Pin the seam allowance from the right side of your skirt in the "ditch" created by the other seam, making sure that you catch the fabric on the other side.

Step 7l

m. Sew all the way around the waistband on the skirt's right side with the zipper foot so that the stitches disappear in the ditch.

n. Press the waistband, then make a buttonhole— one that corresponds to the size of your button— in the left-side tab. Follow your sewing machine's instruction manual to make the buttonhole. Sew your button onto the right side of the waistband, where the fabric lines up beneath the buttonhole.

> **TIP:** *If you are uncomfortable with making a buttonhole, sew on a snap or a hook and eye for a closure instead. Then sew your button on the outside of the flap to give the illusion of a button closure.*

8. Hem Your Skirt

a. Hem your skirt with a 1" (2.5cm) hem allowance: fold the bottom-cut edge ½" (13mm), then fold ½" (13mm) again, hiding the raw edge.

Step 8a

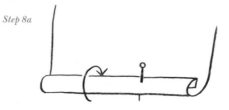

b. If your fabric holds a crease well, press the hem in place; if not, press the hem, then pin it in place as you move around the skirt.

c. Situate your skirt at your machine so that the double-folded hem faces up. Sew over the top edge of the hem. Because the hemline will be visible, try to sew as straight as possible. Make sure to lock-stitch when you start and stop.

> **TIP:** *For less noticeable lockstitches on your finished skirt, start sewing the hem at the center back of your skirt.*

9. Finish Your Skirt

Bring your skirt to the ironing board for a quick, final press and do a thread check, trimming all threads you might have missed while you were sewing.

Now, put on your skirt and check out your amazing work in the mirror. We suggest—at the very least— doing a happy seamstress dance!

A-line

What's Your Angle?

This project is a great way to experiment with mixing color and patterns by incorporating a triangle-shaped panel in contrasting fabric to your skirt.

Materials List

- ☐ A-line pattern (pages 101–102)
- ☐ Basic sewing supplies
- ☐ 1½ yds (1.4m) main fabric
- ☐ 9" (23cm) invisible zipper
- ☐ ½ yd (45.5cm) contrast fabric; or, ½ yd (45.5cm) additional main fabric, if you are using the opposite side as contrast
- ☐ ½" (13mm) wide single-fold bias tape

FABRIC TIP: We used an embroidered, medium-weight cotton with a dotted pattern on the "right side" for the main skirt and a linear pattern on the "wrong side" for the contrast. You can also use two different fabrics; just make sure the weights of both fabrics are similar so that your triangle piece doesn't weigh down that corner of your skirt.

1. Make Your Basic Skirt

Make an A-line skirt following Steps 1–3 in Building Your Basic Skirt (pages 16–17). Once you've completed those steps, cut the fabric into pieces! Specifically, you're going to use a piece cut from the skirt front as the pattern for your contrast triangle.

2. Make Your Triangle

a. Lay the skirt front right side up. Measure 6" (15cm) down the right-side seam and mark the spot with a pin. Now measure 5" (12.5cm) across the hem from the bottom-left corner and mark that spot with another pin.

b. Place a yardstick on the angle created by the two pins. With tailor's chalk, draw a straight line, connecting the pins.

c. To transfer the grain line, fold the skirt front in half lengthwise, wrong sides together, creating a center-front fold. Starting at the bottom of your fold, measure 5" (12.5cm) over and 2" (5cm) up; put a safety pin here, through the top layer only. Repeat twice more, measuring 5" (12.5cm) over from the fold and 2" (5cm) up from each safety pin (for a total of three safety pins).

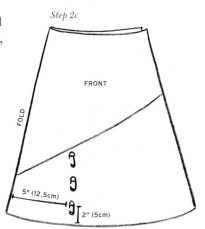

Step 2c

FOLD

FRONT

5" (12.5cm)

2" (5cm)

TIP: *Secure your safety pins so that the tops face up. This will help you keep track of the correct direction of the triangle piece.*

d. Open the skirt front and cut across the chalk line, making sure to cut only one layer of fabric.

NOTE: This triangle will be used as the pattern for your contrast panel, so cut the fabric in a continuous piece.

e. Lay out your contrast fabric in a single layer, right side up; then lay the triangular pattern piece on your contrast fabric, making sure the grain line is parallel to the selvage edge. Pin in place.

NOTE: If you are using the flip side of your main fabric as the contrast triangle, the "wrong side" is now the "right side."

f. Add seam allowance by drawing a line 1¼" (3cm) away from the long angled edge of the pattern.

NOTE: If you don't add the seam allowance, the skirt front will end up being too small.

g. Once you have chalked the seam allowance, extend hem- and side-seam lines to meet the chalk line. The edges curve slightly, so incorporate that curve when extending the lines. Cut out your triangle.

3. Attach Your Triangle

a. Lay your triangle on top of your skirt front, right sides together with cut edges matching up. A triangular tab will stick out ⅝" (16mm) on both sides.

b. Pin the pieces together, then sew a ⅝" (16mm) seam allowance.

Step 3a–b

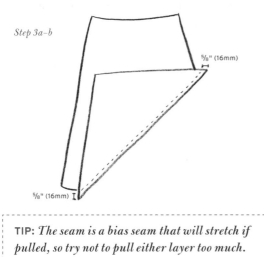

⅝" (16mm)

⅝" (16mm)

> **TIP:** *The seam is a bias seam that will stretch if pulled, so try not to pull either layer too much.*

c. When you're finished, clip the fabric tabs on either side of the seam and finish the edge of the seam with an over-edge zigzag stitch. Press the seam down toward the triangle.

4. Pin-Fit Your Skirt

Match up your skirt front and back, right sides together. Place safety pins every 3" (7.5 cm) along the side seams at a ⅝" (16mm) seam allowance. Try your skirt on and make any adjustments.

Step 4

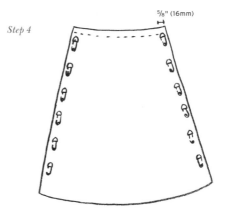

⅝" (16mm)

5. Sew Your Side Seams

If you did not make any changes when pin-fitting, stitch the side seams at a ⅝" (16mm) seam allowance; if you adjusted the safety pins, chalk a vertical mark over each pin, then connect your vertical marks into a continuous line on both sides of your skirt. Sew along these new stitching lines, then trim the seam allowances to ⅝" (16mm). Finish the seam allowances.

6. Sew Your Darts

a. Match up the markings for the dart legs, one on top of the other with the right sides of the fabric together, creating a fold. Keep the fold on your right and the main part of the skirt on your left. Slide the two layers over each other until the dart-tip marking is on the fold. Securely pin the dart down. Repeat for all darts.

b. Lay down a piece of basting tape that's slightly longer than the length of the dart so that the tape's right edge makes a straight line from the cut marks to the dart-tip marking. Sew right next to the tape, starting at the top of the dart where the cuts are, to the dart tip. Repeat for all darts. Press the dart fabric toward the center back of your skirt.

Step 6b

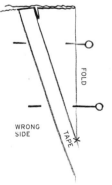

FOLD

WRONG
SIDE

TAPE

7. Sew Your Waistband

a. Measure the circumference of the top of your skirt and add 1¼" (3cm) for a seam allowance. Cut a piece of bias tape to this length.

b. Pin the bias tape right side up to the right side of the top of your skirt: open the zipper and extend one end of the bias tape ⅝" (16mm) past the zipper edge; continue pinning the bias tape around the skirt, covering the skirt's stay-stitching and also slightly overlapping the cut edge, until the tape extends ⅝" (16mm) past the other zipper edge. Sew closely to the bias tape's lower edge. Trim any threads and/or fabric extending past the bias tape no thinner than ⅜" (10mm).

c. Fold the extra bias tape on the ends toward the wrong side of the fabric; then fold the rest of the bias tape toward the wrong side of your skirt, far enough over so that you cannot see it from the outside. Pin the tape in place around your skirt. Sew closely to the bias tape's lower edge, starting and stopping your stitches about ¼" (6mm) from the zipper teeth. Turn your skirt inside out, and press the entire top of the skirt.

Step 7c

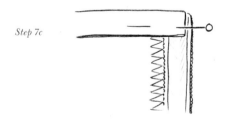

8. Finish Your Skirt

Hem your skirt with a 1" (2.5cm) hem allowance: fold the bottom-cut edge ½" (13mm), then fold ½" (13mm) again, hiding the raw edge; stitch. Press your skirt and do a final thread check.

Rosie the Riveter

For the girl who always has a project going, this skirt is functional and fashionable! Plus, it can be worn with or without the apron.

Materials List

- ☐ A-line pattern (pages 101–102)
- ☐ Basic sewing supplies
- ☐ 1½ yds (1.4m) main fabric
- ☐ 9" (23cm) invisible zipper
- ☐ ½" (13mm) wide single-fold bias tape
- ☐ Apron 1 and 2; hardware loop; and small, medium, and large pocket facing patterns (pages 110–112)
- ☐ ⅜ yd (35cm) contrast fabric
- ☐ ⅜ yd (35cm) medium-weight fusible interfacing
- ☐ 8" (20cm) standard zipper
- ☐ 2 heavy-duty spring clips
- ☐ 2 heavy-duty O-rings

FABRIC TIP: We made our skirt out of a solid-colored, heavy-duty cotton canvas and our apron out of a printed, lightweight cotton. Choose a very sturdy cotton or cotton blend for the skirt; denim is also a good option. Top it off with an apron in a bold print to display your softer side.

1. Make Your Basic Skirt

Complete an A-line skirt following all of the steps in Building Your Basic Skirt (pages 16–22).

2. Make Your Apron

a. Align the register marks (circles) of the two apron patterns and tape them together.

b. Cut out the following:

- Four hardware loops from contrast fabric and interfacing
- Two aprons from contrast fabric
- One apron from main fabric
- Two small pocket facings from contrast fabric and interfacing
- One medium pocket facing from contrast fabric and interfacing
- One large pocket facing from contrast fabric and interfacing.

c. Transfer all pattern markings to your fabric. With small pieces of basting or masking tape, label the apron pieces A, B, and C: apron pieces A and B are cut from the contrast fabric; C is cut from the main fabric.

d. With an iron, fuse interfacing, shiny side down, to the wrong sides of the appropriate fabric pieces (hardware loops and pocket facings).

e. Finish the edges of all four pocket-facing openings with an over-edge zigzag stitch.

f. Pin three pocket facings (two small and one medium) to apron A, right sides together.

Step 2f

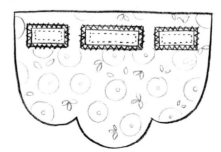

g. Sew around the rectangle indicated by the markings on each pocket-facing piece. Cut a two-sided Y shape inside this stitched rectangle, cutting through both layers (the pocket facing and the apron) and very close to the corners—but not through your stitching line. Repeat for the other two pocket facings.

Step 2g

h. Turn each pocket facing to the inside, creating a rectangular opening; press each one flat.

i. Pin the large pocket facing to apron C, right sides together; then repeat Steps 2g–h.

j. Place the 8" (20cm) zipper right side up (with the zipper pull to the left) centered behind the cut you made in Step 2g. Pin in place.

Step 2j

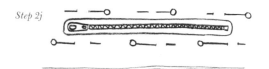

k. With the zipper foot, stitch around the zipper ¼" (6mm) from the pocket opening. Now your apron back is a large zipper pocket.

l. Topstitch around each of the pocket facings on the apron front, ⅜" (10mm) away from the opening in the rectangle.

m. Lay apron A right side up on top of the right side of apron B. Pin the two layers together.

n. Chalk the vertical stitching lines from the pattern to the fabric and sew the layers together to form the pockets.

> **TIP:** *Have fun with the pockets. For example, if you are a painter and would love specially configured pocket spaces for your brushes, sew a bunch of vertical lines onto your pocket facings.*

3. Attach Your Loops and Hardware

a. Fold all four hardware loops in half lengthwise, right sides together. Sew a ⅝" (16mm) seam allowance. Turn right sides out and press.

b. Fold two of the hardware loops in half with short sides (raw edges) together, hiding the seams on the inside. Place a spring clip in the fold of each one.

c. Place each hardware loop facing in toward the body of apron A where indicated; baste in place.

d. Make a fabric sandwich: lay apron C on top of apron A right sides together. Pin all three layers together.

e. Sew the layers together with a ⅝" (16mm) seam allowance, leaving an opening as indicated on the pattern.

> **TIP:** *Because you're working with many layers of fabric, go slowly when sewing over the basted hardware loops.*

f. Clip excess fabric from all curves and corners and turn the fabric sandwich right side out. At the opening, fold your seam allowance in to create a straight edge; press.

g. Topstitch ¼" (6mm) away from the edge all the way around your apron.

h. Slide the two remaining hardware loops through the O-rings, which will attach to your skirt permanently and act as hooks for the apron.

i. Fold the hardware loops right sides together; then sew the cut edges together at ⅝" (16mm). Turn right sides out.

j. With safety pins, pin the hardware loops—one on each side of the skirt—approximately 1¾" (4.5cm) from the top of the back of your skirt. Attach the apron to see if you like the way it hangs. If not, adjust the position of the pinned loops until you achieve the desired fit.

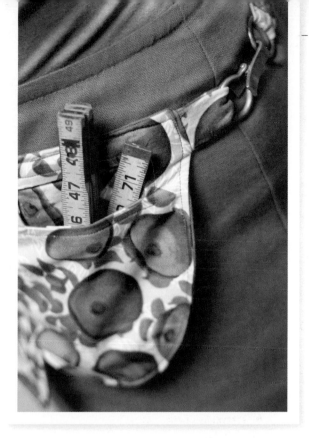

k. Stitch the loops onto your skirt using an *X* pattern, leaving the side nearest the O-rings unstitched for mobility.

Step 3k

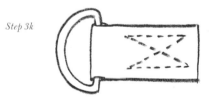

Kind of Sketchy

This little chick isn't daunted by her task, so don't be daunted by making this skirt!

Materials List

☐ A-line pattern (pages 101–102)

☐ Basic sewing supplies

☐ 1½ yds (1.4m) fabric

☐ 9" (23cm) invisible zipper

☐ Images 1, 2, and 3 (pages 107–108). Make 2 copies of image 1 (you'll use one for practice)

☐ Contrast thread

☐ ½" (13mm) wide single-fold bias tape

FABRIC TIP: We used a red denim with yellow thread for optimum eye candy. A heavy-duty cotton or cotton blend with contrasting thread is ideal for this project.

I. Make Your Basic Skirt

Make an A-line skirt following Steps 1–3 in Building Your Basic Skirt (pages 16–17).

VARIATION: Stitch a sketch onto one of your favorite existing skirts for a one-of-a-kind look.

2. Practice Stitching Your Image

When attempting a new technique, it's important to do a practice run to make sure you are comfortable with the process before applying it to your skirt.

a. Pin image 1 right side up to the wrong side of a large fabric scrap.

b. Starting at the bottom of line 1, lower the needle through the paper and stitch until you reach the top of the line. Sharply turn and stitch back down line 2 until you reach its bottom.

NOTE: Don't forget to lockstitch when starting and stopping. You don't want the threads to unravel, or you will lose your image.

c. To create depth, the other side of the ladder is stitched differently: Leave an unstitched space where each rung intersects the ladder support. Starting at the bottom of line 3, follow the vertical line, but this time stop at each rung, lockstitch, lift your needle, and move your work forward to start stitching on the other side of the rung.

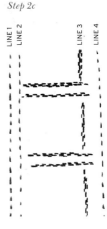

Step 2c

LINE 1 LINE 2 LINE 3 LINE 4

TIP: *If you are using a different image than the one provided, decide which lines should intersect or not to give your image proper depth.*

d. When you reach the top again, sharply turn and stitch straight down line 4. It is not necessary to stop at each rung this time.

e. Clip the threads where the rungs will be sewn.

Image Selection Guidelines

If you're planning to stitch words, you have to reverse the letters or, like in a mirror, the words will read backward. Here are our guidelines for picking an image:

● Choose an easily recognizable silhouette with a bold shape and very few (if any) fussy details.

● Keep in mind that straight lines are much easier to trace than curved lines.

● Don't use an image that's too small. If you are really in love with a small image, enlarge it on a photocopier.

● Feeling fancy? Challenge yourself by using a couple different thread colors.

f. Starting with the bottom rung and paying close attention to where the line begins and ends, stitch each rung, top and bottom, lockstitching when you start and stop.

NOTE: The sewing of the rungs is going to feel very "start and stop." Also, you don't want to cross line 2 or intersect line 4, as doing either will diminish the 3-D look of the ladder.

g. If you're happy with the way your "sketch" looks, you're ready to move on to the real thing. If you think you need a little more practice, grab another fabric scrap and try again.

3. Stitch Your Image

a. Tape images 1 and 2 together, lining up the register marks (circles) to form the ladder.

b. Pin the image right side up to the wrong side of your skirt front. Line up the bottom of the ladder with the unhemmed skirt bottom. The top of the ladder should be $5/8$" (16mm) from the side seam.

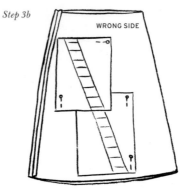

Step 3b

WRONG SIDE

c. Stitch your ladder following Steps 2b–f.

d. Pin image 3 wherever you like. Our chicken is $2^1/4$" (5.5cm) from the ladder and $1^1/2$" (3.8cm) from the bottom of the skirt.

TIP: *Don't place the chicken too low, or you'll cut off her feet when hemming the skirt.*

e. To sew the chicken, start at the tip of the tail, follow all lines, and lockstitch when you start and stop. When you reach the spiral of the eye, release the pressure on your presser foot so that the fabric moves more freely and you don't have to turn the fabric in such a tight circle.

f. Remove the paper from around where you've stitched; you may need to use tweezers to remove some of the smaller pieces.

g. Snip all loose threads on the interior and exterior of the skirt.

4. Pin-Fit Your Skirt

Match up your skirt front and back, right sides together. Place safety pins every 3" (7.5 cm) along the side seams at a ⅝" (16mm) seam allowance. Try on your skirt and make any adjustments.

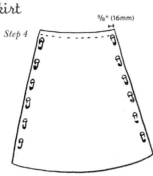

Step 4

⅝" (16mm)

5. Sew Your Side Seams

If you did not make any changes when pin-fitting, stitch the side seams at a ⅝" (16mm) seam allowance; if you adjusted the safety pins, chalk a vertical mark over each pin, then connect your vertical marks into a continuous line on both sides of your skirt. Sew along these new stitching lines, then trim the seam allowances to ⅝" (16mm). Finish the seam allowances.

6. Sew Your Darts

a. Match up the markings for the dart legs, one on top of the other with the right sides of the fabric together, creating a fold. Keep the fold on your right and the main part of the skirt on your left. Slide the two layers over each other until the dart-tip marking is on the fold. Securely pin the dart down. Repeat for all darts.

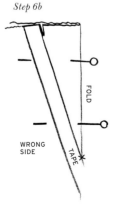

Step 6b

FOLD

WRONG SIDE

TAPE

b. Lay down a piece of basting tape that's slightly longer than the length of the dart so that the tape's right edge makes a straight line from the cut marks to the dart-tip marking. Sew right next to the tape, starting at the top of the dart where the cuts are, to the dart tip. Repeat for all darts. Press the dart fabric toward the center back of your skirt.

7. Sew Your Waistband

a. Measure the circumference of the top of your skirt and add 1¼" (3cm) for a seam allowance. Cut a piece of bias tape to this length.

b. Pin the bias tape right side up to the right side of the top of your skirt: open the zipper and extend one end of the bias tape ⅝" (16mm) past the zipper edge; continue pinning the bias tape around the skirt, covering the skirt's stay-stitching and also slightly overlapping the cut edge, until the tape extends ⅝" (16mm) past the other zipper edge. Sew closely to the bias tape's lower edge. Trim any threads and/or fabric extending past the bias tape no thinner than ⅜" (10mm).

c. Fold the extra bias tape on the ends toward the wrong side of the fabric; then fold the rest of the bias tape toward the wrong side of your skirt, far enough over so that you cannot see it from the outside. Pin the tape in place around your skirt. Sew closely to the bias tape's lower edge, starting and stopping your stitches about ¼" (6mm) from the zipper teeth. Turn your skirt inside out, and press the entire top of the skirt.

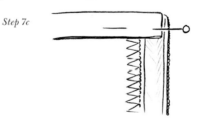

Step 7c

8. Finish Your Skirt

Hem your skirt with a 1" (2.5cm) hem allowance: fold the bottom-cut edge ½" (13mm), then fold ½" (13mm) again, hiding the raw edge; stitch. Press your skirt and do a final thread check.

Mama Mia!

This chic maternity skirt is designed for growth! The combination of a knit waistband and bias-cut skirt maximize stretch and drape.

Materials List

☐ Basic sewing supplies

☐ 1½ yds (1.4m) main fabric

☐ ½ yd (45.5cm) four-way stretch-knit contrast fabric

FABRIC TIP: We used a solid-colored, lightweight denim for the skirt and a striped, four-way stretch knit for the waistband. A lighter fabric will drape better when cut on the bias, and the waistband knit should have a nice stretch and recovery—retaining its original shape. And both fabrics should be fairly neutral in color and pattern so you can pair your skirt with a lot of outfits.

1. Take Your Measurements

Because a pregnant woman's body changes quickly, it's important to measure yourself anew before starting this project. Take two measurements: your hip measurement (wrap the tape around your body at the widest part of your hips), which will be referred to as measurement A, and your side measurement (measure vertically from under your bust to your hip), which will be referred to as measurement B.

TIP: *Do not measure vertically down your center front because, depending on how many months pregnant you are, this measurement may be longer than necessary.*

2. Modify Your Pattern

a. Refer to the A-line pattern (pages 101–102). Draft the front and back pieces based on measurement A (your hip measurement).

Step 2b

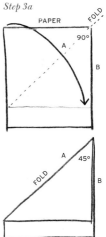

6" (15cm)

b. Once you've cut out the pattern pieces, draw a curved line 6" (15cm) from the top on both pattern pieces.

NOTE: The line will be curved because the top of your skirt is curved.

c. Cut along the curved line on the pattern pieces to accommodate the skirt's new waistband.

3. Change Your Grain Line to a Bias Line

Step 3a

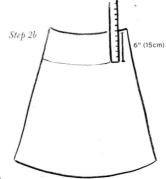

a. The bias line is a 45-degree angle from your true grain line, or your selvage edge. To create a 45-degree angle, fold a piece of letter-sized paper diagonally so that the top edge and the side edge match up. Label the angled edge A and the straight edge B.

b. Line up B with the current grain line on the back-pattern piece. Trace A onto the pattern piece and notate this as the bias line.

c. Cut your main fabric into two pieces. When folded, your skirt-front pattern should fit on one fabric piece and your skirt-back pattern on the other piece. Follow the layout diagrams to pin the pattern pieces onto your fabric:

Step 3c

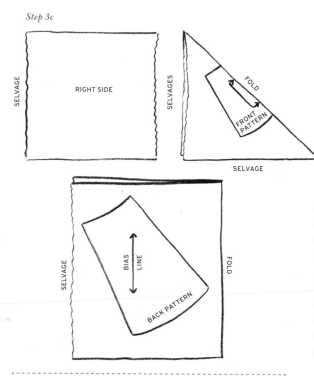

EXAMPLE: Our measurement A was 39" (99cm) and our measurement B was 11" (28cm), so we cut a rectangle that measured 39" by 23¼" (99cm by 59cm).

b. The greatest degree of stretch your fabric has should run in the same direction as measurement A (your hip measurement). Chalk your rectangle measurements right onto your fabric and double-check them before cutting; cut this piece out.

c. Fold your waistband in half right sides together, matching up your measurement B edges; pin together. Using a stretch stitch or zigzag stitch, sew a ⅝" (16mm) seam allowance along the edge to form the center-back seam.

d. Turn the waistband right side out, then fold it in half so that the seam is hidden on the inside and the remaining edges (measurement A) match up with each other; it should look like a tube.

e. Try the waistband on so that the seam is at your center back and the top of the waistband comes up to about your bustline.

TIP: *If you want your finished skirt to be longer, extend the hemline, then extend the side seams to meet the new hemline. Make these changes before cutting out your fabric.*

---

d. Cut out your fabric.

4. Make Your Waistband

a. For the waistband, cut out a rectangle the length of measurement A by the width of measurement B multiplied by 2, plus 1¼" (3cm) for seam allowance: A by [2(B) + 1¼" (3cm)].

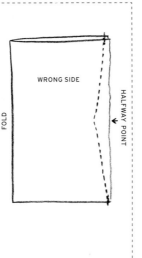

f. Once your waistband fits well, trim the seam allowance to ⅝" (16mm). Press the seam open, turn right side out, and set this piece aside.

5. Sew Your Skirt Body

Sew the center-back seam at a ⅝" (16mm) seam allowance and finish the edges; then sew both side seams at a ⅝" (16mm) seam allowance and finish the edges.

NOTE: If your skirt seems a little big after you finish the seams, that's fine. You'll want to be able to grow a bit in this skirt!

6. Sew Your Skirt Together

a. Quarter your waistband: Fold it in half with the back seam on one side and the center front on the opposite side. Place a pin at the cut edge of the center front. Bring the center-front pin to the center-back seam to create your side-seam marks; place pins in both of these spots. You should have three pins and one seam that represent the quarters of the waistband.

b. Repeat Step 6a with the top of your skirt body.

c. With the right sides of the waistband and skirt body together, match up your quarter marks, starting with the back seams. Now match up the center front of the waistband with the center front of the skirt body; then match up the left and right sides, (these may not coincide with the side seams). Pin together all three layers (two from the folded waistband and one from the skirt body).

Step 6c

NOTE: You might need to do some easing on the part of either the waistband or the skirt, but since you're working with a stretch fabric and a bias cut, you should be able to manipulate the layers until they fit together.

d. Using a stretch stitch or zigzag stitch, sew the waistband to the skirt body with a ⅝" (16mm) seam allowance all the way around the pinned area.

e. Finish the seam with an over-edge zigzag stitch. Press the seam down toward the skirt body.

7. Finish Your Skirt

Hem your skirt with a 1" (2.5cm) hem allowance: fold the bottom-cut edge ½" (13mm), then fold ½" (13mm) again, hiding the raw edge; stitch. Press your skirt and do a final thread check.

Two-Layer Jack-Up

This project is all about layering fabrics and adding texture. You will also learn how to make French seams.

Materials List

- ☐ A-line pattern (pages 101–102)
- ☐ Basic sewing supplies
- ☐ 1½ yds (1.4m) sheer (outer shell) fabric + ½ yd (45.5cm) additional fabric
- ☐ 1½ yds (1.4m) opaque (lining) fabric
- ☐ ½" (13mm) wide single-fold bias tape
- ☐ Embroidery floss (in contrast color to sheer fabric)
- ☐ Hand-sewing needle with a large eye

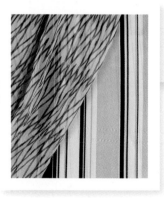

FABRIC TIP: We paired a striped, opaque silk for the lining with a geometric-patterned, sheer silk chiffon for the outer shell. This project is a great opportunity to play with print over print and work with super sheer silks. When choosing fabrics, try to find two bold prints that look interesting layered over one another.

1. Make Your Basic Skirts

a. For the lining (the opaque fabric), make an A-line skirt following Steps 1–6 in Building Your Basic Skirt (pages 16–20).

b. For the outer shell (the sheer fabric), follow Steps 1–2 (page 16) with an exception: Make this layer 10" (25cm) longer in both the front and the back. Measure down 10" (25 cm) from the bottom of the pattern, draw a line on your fabric with tailor's chalk, and extend the side seams to meet your new hemline.

c. For the outer shell, skip to Steps 4–6 in Building Your Basic Skirt (pages 18–20). However, when sewing your side seams, make French seams: Pin your side-seam allowances wrong sides together and stitch a ¼" (6mm) seam allowance. Press your seams toward the back of your skirt, then fold the right sides together and stitch a ⅜" (10mm) seam allowance.

d. Pin the wrong sides of your outer-shell skirt backs together at the center-back seam. Mark where the zipper would end on the seam by laying the outer shell next to the lining, which already has the zipper sewn into it.

Step 1d

> **TIP:** *Mark this spot with two pins set very close to each other to emphasize the point at which you will begin the French seam for the center back.*

WRONG SIDES TOGETHER

CENTER-BACK SEAM

e. Make a French seam (see Step 1c) from the double-pin mark, down. Leave the zipper area open for the time being.

2. Sew Your Skirt Layers Together

a. Join the wrong side of the outer shell to the right side of the lining at the zipper: turn the outer shell fabric under two times—using up the allotted ⅝" (16mm) seam allowance—then pin it to the lining fabric right next to the zipper. Repeat the pinning on the other side of the zipper.

Step 2b

b. Unzip the zipper. With the zipper foot, topstitch through both the outer shell and the lining, making sure not to catch any of the zipper or zipper tape in the stitching.

> **TIP:** *This line of stitching will show on the finished skirt, so try to sew as neatly as possible.*

NOTE: The reason you are attaching the layers in this way is to allow them to hang separately below the zipper.

c. Match up the tops of your two skirt layers and baste them together all the way around the top with a ⅜" (10mm) seam allowance.

3. Sew Your Waistband

a. Measure the circumference of the top of your skirt and add 1¼" (3cm) for a seam allowance. Cut a piece of bias tape to this length.

b. Pin the bias tape right side up to the right side of the top of your skirt: open the zipper and extend one end of the bias tape ⅝" (16mm) past the zipper edge; continue pinning the bias tape around the skirt, covering the skirt's stay-stitching and also slightly overlapping the cut edge, until the tape extends ⅝" (16mm) past the other zipper edge. Sew closely to the bias tape's lower edge. Trim any threads and/or fabric extending past the bias tape no thinner than ⅜" (10mm).

c. Fold the extra bias tape on the ends toward the wrong side of the fabric; then fold the rest of the bias tape toward the wrong side of your skirt, far enough over so that you cannot see it from the outside. Pin the tape in place around your skirt. Sew closely to the bias tape's lower edge, starting and stopping your stitches about ¼" (6mm) from the zipper teeth. Turn your skirt inside out, and press the entire top of the skirt.

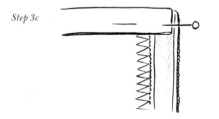

Step 3c

4. Finish Your Skirt

Hem your skirt with a 1" (2.5cm) hem allowance: fold the bottom-cut edge ½" (13mm), then fold ½" (13mm) again, hiding the raw edge. Press your skirt and do a final thread check.

Tips on Hemming Silk

Many types of silk can be very difficult to hem because of their slippery nature and tendency to fray. This hemming process takes a few steps, but you'll be happy with the finished product.

1. Sew ½" (13mm) away from the bottom of your unfinished hem.

2. Fold at that stitching line, then sew again next to the fold.

3. Trim down any fabric that extends past the second line of stitching.

4. Fold again toward the wrong side at ½" (13mm); stitch again.

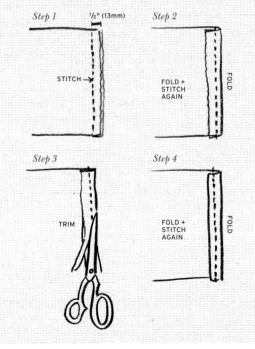

5. Tack Up Your Skirt

This part of the process is very free-form and organic. Instead of telling you exactly where to tack up your skirt, we are going to give you a few basic guidelines. Refer to the photos of our skirt, or take your tacking-up in a different direction.

> **TIP:** *You don't want to create bulk around your hips, so start tacking up your fabric 10" (25cm) or so from the top of your skirt.*

a. Starting about 10" (25cm) from the top of your skirt, pinch a small amount of the outer-shell fabric between your fingers and fold it up toward the waistband. Pin in place through the bottom layer. Moving down your skirt, continue pinching and folding, making sure to pin the two layers together and that you are happy with the placement of your tack-ups. If you'd like to change anything, do it now, before you secure the folds.

NOTE: Pinch and fold only the top layer of fabric.

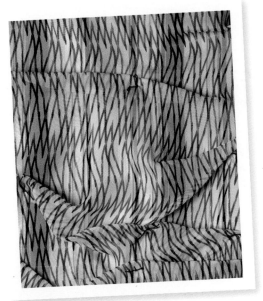

b. Thread two strands of embroidery floss through a hand-sewing needle for the tack-up tying technique (don't knot the thread): start by pushing the needle through the front of your skirt at your tack mark, going through both layers of fabric; then pull the thread back to the front, right next to where you pushed it through. Leave about a 3" (7.5cm) tail of floss on the front of your skirt.

> **TIP:** *Catch a small amount of fabric for a subtle tack-up, or grab more for a dramatic look.*

c. Take the two tails of floss and tie them together three times, securing them with a simple knot. Leave about 1" (2.5cm) of floss tails hanging for more visual interest and texture.

Step 5c

d. Repeat Steps 5b–c at each of your tack-up spots.

> **TIP:** *If you prefer not to see the threads, do your tying on the inside of the skirt.*

NOTE: Depending on how you did your tack-ups, the two layers of your skirt may not be even; this is part of the design. It's fine if the top layer is slightly longer (for a sheer detail) or slightly shorter (so the lining peeks out).

VARIATION: Have a skirt in your closet that needs a makeover? Create a sheer overlay that is longer than the original and try the tack-up technique.

Outside the Box Pleat

Put on your thinking cap because this skirt requires some calculation, but once you get the hang of it, you'll be incorporating these pleats into all of your skirts.

Materials List

- ☐ A-line pattern (pages 101–102)
- ☐ Basic sewing supplies
- ☐ 1½ yds (1.4m) main fabric + ½ yd (45.5cm) additional fabric
- ☐ 9" (23cm) invisible zipper
- ☐ ½" (13mm) wide single-fold bias tape
- ☐ ¼ yd (23cm) contrast fabric
- ☐ Calculator (optional)

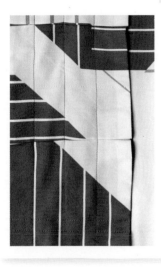

FABRIC TIP: We used a geometric-patterned, lightweight silk and cotton blend for the main fabric and a solid silk for the contrast. Choose a fabric that is lightweight for easy pleating. This skirt looks great in a solid fabric, too.

1. Make Your Basic Skirt

Make an A-line skirt, following Steps 1–7f in Building Your Basic Skirt (pages 16–21). You will be adding a 5½" (14cm) panel to the bottom, so you may want to make your skirt body shorter than usual. (Don't hem it.)

2. Make Your Panels

a. To determine the length of the vertical panel, measure down the front of your skirt from the top to the unfinished hem; call this measurement A.

b. Divide measurement A by 5 (the pleats will be spaced 5", or 12.5cm, apart) to figure out the number of box pleats you'll be making. Call this measurement B; if you don't get an even number, round up: A / 5" (12.5cm) = B

EXAMPLE: Our skirt's measurement A was 12³⁄₄" (32.5cm): 12³⁄₄" (32.5cm)/5" (12.5cm) = 2.5 pleats. We rounded B up to 3 pleats.

c. Since each pleat uses 4" (10cm) of fabric, multiply measurement B by 4" (10cm) to get the amount of fabric you'll need for the pleats. Call this measurement C: B x 4" (10cm) = C.

EXAMPLE: Our measurement B was 3 pleats: 3 pleats x 4" (10cm) = 12" (30.5cm).

d. Add measurement C to measurement A, plus ⁵⁄₈" (16mm) for a seam allowance. This will be the length of your vertical panel: C + A + ⁵⁄₈" (16mm) = vertical panel length.

EXAMPLE: Our measurement C was 12" (30.5cm), and our measurement A was 12³⁄₄" (32.5cm): 12" (30.5cm) + 12³⁄₄" (32.5cm) + ⁵⁄₈" (16mm) = 25³⁄₈" (64.5cm). The length of our vertical panel is 25³⁄₈" (64.5cm).

The width of the vertical panel is the same for everyone at 6¾" (17cm), including seam allowance.

e. Cut two pieces of fabric—one out of your main fabric and one from your contrast fabric—that measure the length of your vertical panel by a width of 6¾" (17cm).

EXAMPLE: Cut out, our fabric measured 25³⁄₈" (64.5cm) long by 6¾" (17cm) wide.

f. To determine the length of the horizontal panel, measure the circumference of the bottom of your skirt and record it as measurement D.

g. Divide measurement D by 5 (the pleats will be spaced 5", or 12.5cm, apart) to get measurement E, the number of pleats on your panel:
D / 5" (12.5cm) = E.

EXAMPLE: Our measurement D was 50" (127cm): 50" (127cm) / 5" (12.5cm) = 10 pleats. If your number does not come out even, round up the number of pleats to the next whole number. (Don't worry! We'll show you how to make it fit even if your numbers aren't exact.)

h. Each pleat needs 4" (10cm) of fabric, so multiply measurement E by 4" (10cm) to get the amount of fabric you'll need for the pleats. Call this measurement F: E x 4" = F.

EXAMPLE: Our measurement E was 10: 10 x 4" (10cm) = 40" (101.5cm).

i. Add measurement F to measurement D. This will be the length of your horizontal panel: F + D = horizontal panel length.

EXAMPLE: Our measurement F was 40" (101.5cm), and our measurement D was 50" (127cm): 40" (101.5cm) + 50" (127cm) = 90" (2.3m). The length of our horizontal panel is 90" (2.3m).

The width of the horizontal panel is the same for everyone at 6¾" (17cm), including hem allowance.

j. Cut out one piece of your main fabric that measures the length of your horizontal panel by a width of 6¾" (17cm). Your fabric is most likely not wide enough to accommodate a consecutive piece of fabric that measures the length of your horizontal panel. Connect pieces and make seams where necessary; for every panel you cut out, add to its length a 1¼" (3cm) seam allowance.

EXAMPLE: We cut three pieces of fabric a total length of 93¾" (2.4m). When the three pieces were stitched together with a ⅝" (16mm) seam allowance, the piece equaled 90" (2.3m).

3. Attach Your Vertical Panel

a. Face together and pin the right sides of your two pieces of fabric for the vertical panel.

b. Stitch down both long sides and across the top edge with a ⅝" (16mm) seam allowance, leaving the bottom edge open.

c. Clip excess fabric from the corners and flip the panel right side out. Press the fabric to get nice clean edges and corners.

d. Chalk a vertical line down the exact center of your panel.

NOTE: Your panel is 5½" (14cm) wide, so the center will be 2¾" (7cm) from each edge.

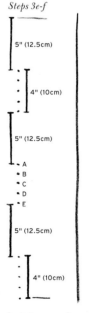

Steps 3e-f

5" (12.5cm)

4" (10cm)

5" (12.5cm)

A
B
C
D
E

5" (12.5cm)

4" (10cm)

e. Map out your box pleats on this center line: For the first pleat, measure down 5" (12.5cm) from the top of the panel and make a dot mark. Measure 1" (2.5cm) from this mark and make another dot mark; make a dot mark every 1" (2.5cm) until you have five marks total. Then measure 5" (12.5cm) and repeat this process until you reach the bottom of your panel.

f. From top to bottom, label the five dot marks for each pleat A–E.

g. Chalk a vertical line down the center of your skirt front.

h. Line up the top edges and vertical lines of your panel and skirt front, then pin the contrast side of the vertical panel to the right side of your skirt front. Pin the two layers together until you are 1" (2.5cm) away from the first dot mark.

i. To make the first box pleat, fold dot A down to meet dot C and pin in place—the extra fabric should lie behind the fold; this is the first half of the box pleat. For the second half of the pleat, fold dot E up to meet dot C. The two folds should butt up against each other without overlapping or leaving a gap. Pin the pleat down. Repeat for all pleats.

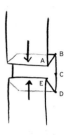

Step 3i

NOTE: When you reach the bottommost pleat, don't worry if you have a bit of excess fabric that is longer than your skirt front. You will trim that off later.

j. Sew down the center of the panel to secure the pleats to your skirt front.

k. Add two more lines of stitching 1⅝" (4cm) to the left and to the right of the center line of stitching.

l. Trim any extra fabric hanging below the bottom of your skirt front, so it is even with the bottom edge.

m. Use a basting stitch at a ⅜" (10mm) seam allowance to attach the bottom edge of the panel to your skirt.

4. Attach Your Horizontal Panel

a. Sew your horizontal-panel pieces into a continuous piece (a tube) by joining the short sides together with a $^5/_8$" (16mm) seam allowance.

b. Finish the edges of the seam allowances with an over-edge zigzag stitch, then press them open so they lie flat.

c. It's much easier to hem the panel now, before it's sewn to your skirt. Fold the bottom (long) edge $^3/_8$" (10mm) twice to create your hem. Stitch in place, then press.

d. Starting anywhere on the horizontal panel, make a small clip with your scissors into the unhemmed side. Measure 1" (2.5cm) away from this clip and make another clip; make a clip every 1" (2.5cm) until you have five clips total. Then measure 5" (12.5cm) from this "clip cluster" and repeat this process all the way around your horizontal panel.

NOTE: If you have an uneven amount of fabric left at the end, don't worry. We will address that later.

e. Pin the right sides together, with the clipped edge of the horizontal panel lining up with the bottom edge of your skirt.

NOTE: Start pinning at the center back of your skirt so that any adjustments that need to be made at the end will be in the back of your skirt.

f. To make the first box pleat, fold in the same manner as you folded the pleat in Step 3i; but this time, fold from side to side rather than up and down.

TIP: *Once you get all the way around your skirt, you may find that you need to make the last pleat slightly larger or smaller: fold a bit more or less fabric into each side of the pleat to get it to lie flat.*

g. Once you have pinned all the box pleats, sew all layers together with a $^5/_8$" (16mm) seam allowance; finish the seam-allowance edges together with an over-edge zigzag stitch.

NOTE: You caught the unfinished edge of the vertical panel when attaching the horizontal panel.

h. Press the seam allowance up toward the skirt body, then topstitch $^1/_4$" (6mm) from the edge of this seam allowance; this will keep the seam allowance in place and help it lie nice and flat.

Step 4h

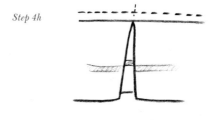

TIP: *We prefer not to press the horizonal-panel pleats flat because they lose their volume.*

Zip It Up

Instead of using a pattern, this free-form project relies on a draping technique that you fit right on your body. Try making the skirt our way the first time, then reinvent it for your next attempt.

Materials List

☐ Basic sewing supplies

☐ 1½ yds (1.4m) 60" (152.5cm) wide fabric

☐ 9" (23cm) invisible zipper

☐ ½" (13mm) wide single-fold bias tape

FABRIC TIP: We used a solid-colored polyester satin-backed crepe. We wanted this skirt to be interesting without being too delicate. Look for a drapey fabric that has a matte and a shiny side that looks good from both sides.

I. Make Your Basic Skirt

a. Using the entire width of your fabric, cut two pieces that measure the desired length of your skirt, plus 1⅜" (3.5cm).

b. Follow Step 3 in Building Your Basic Skirt (page 17).

TIP: *Make the selvage edges of your fabric pieces into the center-back seam; that way, the edges won't fray or need to be finished.*

2. Make Your Pleats

a. Moving 2" (5cm) out from the center back on both the left and right sides, measure and place a pin every 1" (2.5cm) for 8" (20cm), for a total of eighteen pins (nine on each side). Label your pins A–I.

b. Fold your fabric into three pleats, moving away from the center back. Fold A to C, D to F, and G to I. (The diagram, below, shows how to fold the left-back side; reverse it for the right-back side.) Pin the pleats in place.

Step 2b

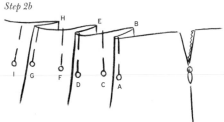

c. Now measure 1" (2.5cm) over from your pleats on both sides of your skirt, and place a pin every 1" (2.5cm) for 8" (20cm), for a total of eighteen pins (nine on each side). Label your pins A–I.

d. Fold a second set of three pleats in the opposite direction from Step 2b; this time, fold I to G, F to D, and C to A.

Step 2d

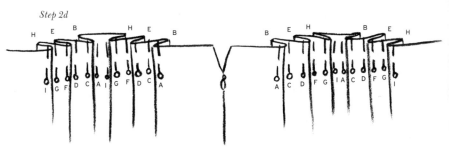

e. To stitch the pleats in place, sew horizontally across your pleats on each side of your skirt back at ⅜" (10mm) from the top edge.

NOTE: This might look like a lot of fabric now, but the pleats will be stitched down later.

3. Shape Your Skirt

Try on your skirt by centering the zipper at the back and wrapping the fabric around you toward the front. Bring the two sides of fabric together about 3" (7.5cm) left of your center front. Your skirt will dip down a bit at this meeting point because of the fabric's weight; this is part of the design. Choose the most flattering and comfortable spot on your body for the skirt to sit—your natural waist, hips, or in-between. Pin the two layers, wrong sides together, where you want your seam to be.

Step 3

NOTE: Leave the pin in place and unzip the zipper to take off your skirt.

4. Sew Your Waistband

a. Cut two pieces of bias tape; each piece should be the length from center back, measuring from each side of the zipper to the pin in front, plus 1¼" (3cm) for seam allowance.

NOTE: Because the front pin is positioned off-center, the two pieces of bias tape will be different lengths.

b. Open up the front of your skirt; make sure to mark the placement of your pin on both fabric layers before removing it.

c. Fold under the end of your first piece of bias tape ⁵/₈" (16mm) to the tape's wrong side for a clean edge; pin it to the right side of the skirt's top, starting at the front-pin mark and ending at the back zipper, also folding under the end ⁵/₈" (16mm) to the tape's wrong side. Repeat with the other piece of bias tape. Sew closely to the lower edge of both pieces of bias tape.

d. Before folding the bias tape to the wrong side of your skirt, trim the extra fabric on the front seam: measure 12½" (31.5cm) out from the pin mark on both pieces of fabric; this will be the length of each of your front pieces.

e. Trim the excess fabric—beyond 12½" (31.5cm)—straight down.

f. Hem the side edges, turning the fabric under ¼" (6mm) twice toward the right side; then hem the top edges that extend past the bias tape, also turning fabric under ¼" (6mm) twice toward the right side of the fabric.

g. Fold the bias tape toward the wrong side of your skirt, far enough over so that you cannot see it from the outside. Pin the tape in place around your skirt. Sew closely to the lower edge of both pieces of bias tape, starting and stopping your stitches about ¼" (6mm) from the zipper teeth. Turn your skirt inside out, and press the entire top of the skirt.

5. Hem Your Skirt

Hem your skirt with a 1" (2.5cm) hem allowance: fold the bottom-cut edge ½" (13mm), then fold ½" (13mm) again, hiding the raw edge; stitch. Press your skirt and do a final thread check.

NOTE: Finish your hem before closing up the front seam.

6. Finish Your Skirt

a. Match up your front panels wrong sides together. Measure over 5" (12.5cm) from the hemmed side edges along the bottom of the skirt and chalk a mark. Now chalk a mark on the top edges of the front panels where the bias tape ends. Draw a diagonal line, connecting the top and bottom marks.

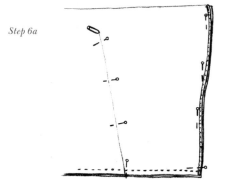

Step 6a

b. Stitch on that line from top to bottom, then press the seam open.

c. On the back of your skirt, pin the pleats down 5½" (14cm) from the top of your skirt.

d. Stitch back and forth over the pleats, ⅜" (10mm) away from the next line of stitching. Stitch fifteen lines in a continuous line, pivoting at the ends to sew down a few stitches, then pivoting again to start the next row. Repeat on the other side of the zipper.

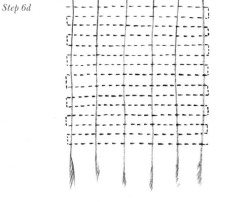

Step 6d

Pencil

A Stitch in Time

Looking for a way to make a simple skirt a standout skirt?
A few lines of stitching detail can take a skirt from just plain fine to fabulous.

Materials List

- ☐ Pencil pattern (pages 103–104)
- ☐ Basic sewing supplies
- ☐ 1½ yds (1.4m) fabric
- ☐ 9" (23cm) invisible zipper
- ☐ 7 pieces 20" (51cm) long yarn (for creating your design)
- ☐ Thread (in a contrast color to your fabric)
- ☐ ½" (13mm) wide single-fold bias tape

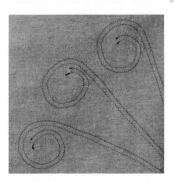

FABRIC TIP: We used a solid-colored, medium-weight wool, but you can use any type of solid-colored, medium-weight fabric, especially if you don't want it to be a winter skirt.

THREAD TIP: Think about what color thread you want to use for your stitching detail. When choosing thread, you can go either high or low contrast.

1. Make Your Basic Skirt

Make a Pencil skirt following Steps 1–3 in Building Your Basic Skirt (pages 16–17), then skip to Step 6 (pages 19–20) to sew darts in your skirt front and back.

2. Lay Out Your Design

It's much easier to work with flat fabric, so stitch your design before your skirt is sewn together.

NOTE: We used a zigzag stitch on our skirt, but experiment on a fabric scrap with the variety of stitches available on your machine to see which you like best.

Steps 2a-b

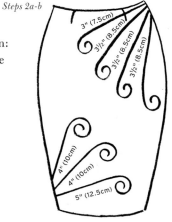

a. Lay your skirt front wrong side up and use the yarn to create your pattern: Starting at the top-right corner, secure a piece of yarn with a pin, then run the yarn out from the side edge; at 10" (25cm) out, the yarn should be 3" (7.5cm) from the top of your skirt. At this point, shape the yarn to complete the curlicue of the design. The four subsequent lines of yarn should be 3½" (8.5cm) from the previous line, when 10" (25cm) out.

b. For the lower detail, start at the bottom-left corner, secure a piece of yarn with a pin, then run the yarn out from the side edge; at 10" (25cm) out, the yarn should be 5" (12.5cm) from the bottom of your skirt. At this point, shape the yarn to complete the curlicue of the design. The 2nd and 3rd lines of yarn should be 4" (10cm) from the previous line, when 10" (25cm) out.

c. Pin the yarn pieces to your skirt.

d. Use tailor's chalk to sketch the design alongside the yarn; these chalk lines will be your stitching lines. Remove the yarn.

3. Stitch Your Design

a. Stitch over the chalk lines, making sure to lock-stitch at the beginning and end of each line. Check out your skirt from the front side every now and again to make sure everything looks good.

> **TIP:** *If you are feeling inspired, stitch a design on the back of your skirt, too.*

b. To make the detail a little more noticeable, run a second line of stitching next to the first, approximately ⅛" (3mm) away.

NOTE: **If you like the way the single line of stitching looks, don't feel that you need to add the second line.**

c. Press your skirt, running over the stitching lines to make them lie flat.

4. Pin-Fit Your Skirt

Match up your skirt front and back, right sides together. Place safety pins every 3" (7.5 cm) along the side seams at a ⅝" (16mm) seam allowance. Try on your skirt and make any adjustments.

5. Sew Your Side Seams

If you did not make any changes when pin-fitting, stitch the side seams at a ⅝" (16mm) seam allowance; if you adjusted the safety pins, chalk a vertical mark over each pin, then connect your vertical marks into a continuous line on both sides of your skirt. Sew along these new stitching lines, then trim the seam allowances to ⅝" (16mm). Finish the seam allowances.

6. Sew Your Waistband

a. Measure the circumference of the top of your skirt and add 1¼" (3cm) for a seam allowance. Cut a piece of bias tape to this length.

b. Pin the bias tape right side up to the right side of the top of your skirt: open the zipper and extend one end of the bias tape ⅝" (16mm) past the zipper edge; continue pinning the bias tape around the skirt, covering the skirt's stay-stitching and also slightly overlapping the cut edge, until the tape extends ⅝" (16mm) past the other zipper edge. Sew closely to the bias tape's lower edge. Trim any threads and/or fabric extending past the bias tape no thinner than ⅜" (10mm).

c. Fold the extra bias tape on the ends toward the wrong side of the fabric; then fold the rest of the bias tape toward the wrong side of your skirt, far enough over so that you cannot see it from the outside. Pin the tape in place around your skirt. Sew closely to the bias tape's lower edge, starting and stopping your stitches about ¼" (6mm) from the zipper teeth. Turn your skirt inside out and press the entire top of the skirt.

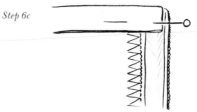

Step 6c

7. Finish Your Skirt

Hem your skirt with a 1" (2.5cm) hem allowance: fold the bottom-cut edge ½" (13mm), then fold ½" (13mm) again, hiding the raw edge; stitch. Press your skirt and do a final thread check.

VARIATION: Stitching a design is a great way to customize a store-bought skirt. Just be careful not to sew both layers of the skirt together!

Cute as a Button

Sometimes you need a place to show off some of the cute buttons in your ever-growing button collection. This project does just that, using those lovely little gems to add a flattering vertical detail to a simple skirt.

Materials List

- ☐ Pencil pattern
  (pages 103-104)

- ☐ Basic sewing supplies

- ☐ 1½ yds (1.4m) main fabric

- ☐ 9" (23cm) invisible zipper

- ☐ ½" (13mm) wide single-fold
  bias tape

- ☐ Paper

- ☐ Scallop template (page 108)

- ☐ ¼ yd (23cm) contrast fabric

- ☐ ¼ yd (23cm) lining fabric

- ☐ 6-10 buttons
  (1 for each scallop)

FABRIC TIP: Our fabric is
actually a curtain panel from
the 1940s, but any lightweight
cotton or cotton blend with a
large print will do. Couple
it with a slightly textured
solid-colored fabric to ground
the print and feature the
buttons; our solid contrast
is microfiber.

1. Make Your Basic Skirt

Make a Pencil skirt following Steps 1–6 in Building Your Basic Skirt
(pages 16–20).

2. Make Your Placket

a. Measure the vertical length of your skirt front. Each scallop takes
3" (7.5cm) of fabric, so divide the skirt-front measurement by 3. The
result equals the number of scallops you need to make for your placket.
Round up to an even number—it's better to have more fabric than less.

EXAMPLE: Our skirt-front length was 25" (63.5cm): 25" (63.5cm) / 3"
(7.5cm) = 8.3, which we rounded up to 9 scallops.

b. To make your placket pattern, you need a piece of paper that's at least
the length of your skirt front and as wide as the scallop template. (If you
don't have paper long enough to accommodate the pattern, tape a few pieces
together.) With a pencil and a yardstick, draw a straight line that is the
length of your skirt front down one side of the paper.

c. Fold under the bottom of the scallop template
on the fold line, then line up the straight side edge
of the template with the top of the straight line
you've just drawn. Trace around the template and
transfer the two dot markings to the paper.

Steps 2c–e

d. To create the second scallop, fold under the
top of the scallop template along the fold lines, then
line up the top-folded edge with the bottom of the
first scallop.

e. Sketch around the template and transfer the pattern's dot markings.
Repeat this process for all scallops except the bottommost scallop;
for this scallop, unfold the bottom fold of the template, then sketch
around it and transfer the dot markings. Cut out your placket pattern.

f. Cut one placket out of contrast fabric, with the scallops of the pattern
facing right; flip the pattern over and cut one out of lining fabric. Transfer
the dot markings to your fabric.

g. Pin both placket pieces right sides together; sew a ⅝" (16mm) seam
allowance down the straight side and the scalloped side, leaving the top
and bottom open. When sewing the scalloped side, pivot your stitches
at each dot marking to create a nice even curve.

TIP: *To pivot most efficiently at the dot markings, stop sewing, leave the needle in the fabric, lift the presser foot, and turn your work, remembering to realign your edge at ⅝" (16mm). Put your presser foot back down.*

h. Clip the curves and cut into the dot markings without clipping the stitches.

Step 2h

i. Turn the fabric right side out and press the placket neat and flat.

3. Attach Your Placket

a. Line up the top of the placket with the top of your skirt (lining side of placket to right side of skirt), with the placket centered on your skirt front; the scallops should face to the right. Pin in place.

b. Topstitch the straight edge of the placket at a ⅛" (3mm) seam allowance.

c. Baste the top and bottom of the placket to your skirt with a ⅜" (10mm) seam allowance. The placket may hang over the bottom edge of your skirt; trim the extra fabric so the pieces are even.

NOTE: The top and bottom of the placket will be sewn into the stitches of the waistband and hem, which will keep the placket from flapping around.

4. Sew Your Waistband

a. Measure the circumference of the top of your skirt and add 1¼" (3cm) for a seam allowance. Cut a piece of bias tape to this length.

b. Pin the bias tape right side up to the right side of the top of your skirt: open the zipper and extend one end of the bias tape ⅝" (16mm) past the zipper edge; continue pinning the bias tape around the skirt, covering the skirt's stay-stitching and also slightly overlapping the cut edge, until the tape extends ⅝" (16mm) past the other zipper edge. Sew closely to the bias tape's lower edge. Trim any threads and/or fabric extending past the bias tape no thinner than ⅜" (10mm).

c. Fold the extra bias tape on the ends toward the wrong side of the fabric; then fold the rest of the bias tape toward the wrong side of your skirt, far enough over so that you cannot see it from the outside. Pin the tape in place around your skirt. Sew closely to the bias tape's lower edge, starting and stopping your stitches about ¼" (6mm) from the zipper teeth. Turn your skirt inside out, and press the entire top of the skirt.

Step 4c

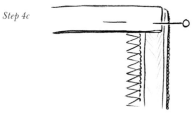

5. Finish Your Skirt

Hem your skirt with a 1" (2.5cm) hem allowance: fold the bottom-cut edge ½" (13mm), then fold ½" (13mm) again, hiding the raw edge; stitch. Press your skirt and do a final thread check.

6. Sew Your Buttons

When sewing the buttons on, you will also secure the placket to the skirt. Mark the center of each scallop, then hand-sew a button in place through all the fabric layers, making sure your stitches are tight and secure.

Don't Hem Me In

The hem of a skirt is a great place to inject a little personality while keeping the rest of the skirt smooth and sexy. Follow our asymmetrical hem or design your own.

Materials List

- ☐ Pencil pattern (pages 103–104)
- ☐ Basic sewing supplies
- ☐ 1½ yds (1.4m) outer-shell fabric + ⅓ yd (30.5cm) additional fabric
- ☐ 1½ yds (1.4m) lining fabric
- ☐ 9" (23cm) invisible zipper
- ☐ ½" (13mm) wide single-fold bias tape
- ☐ Paper
- ☐ Sculpted-hem (1–5) patterns (pages 113–117)

FABRIC TIP: We love to mix dots and stripes, so we used a large-eyelet cotton over a striped cotton. This skirt would also look amazing as one layer in a solid-colored, opaque fabric; remember, though, to pick something light- to medium-weight, as the hem is self-lined.

1. Make Your Basic Skirts

a. Make two Pencil skirts —the outer shell and the lining—following Step 1 in Building Your Basic Skirt (page 16).

b. Pin the right side of the lining to the wrong side of the outer shell. From this point forward, treat the two layers as one.

c. Return to Step 2 (page 16) and stay-stitch the top of your skirt through both layers, making sure they are nice and flat.

d. Continue with Steps 3–7f (pages 17–21).

2. Make Your Sculpted-Hem Pattern

a. Measure your skirt's circumference 4½" (11.5cm) up from the bottom.

b. Align the register marks (circles) of the five sculpted-hem patterns and tape them together; then measure the pattern's total length. If the pattern is 1¼" (3cm) longer than your skirt's circumference measurement, it's the correct size and you can move on to Step 3 (page 62). If your pattern is longer or shorter than your skirt measurement, follow the instructions below.

c. If you need to make your hem longer or shorter than the sculpted-hem pattern, cut along the lines down the center of each scallop.

d. To make your new sculpted-hem pattern, you need a piece of paper that is at least 5" (12.5cm) wide by the length of your hem measurement, plus 1¼" (3cm) for the seam allowance. (If you don't have paper long enough to accommodate the pattern, tape a few pieces together.)

EXAMPLE: Our hem measurement was 38¼" (97cm) long—39½" (100.5cm) with the 1¼" (3cm) seam allowance—so we cut out a rectangular piece of paper that was 5" by 39½" (12.5cm by 100.5cm).

e. Arrange the cut scallops on your rectangular piece of paper until the desired length is achieved. Space the pattern pieces apart to make the scallops longer (below left), or overlap the pieces to make the scallops shorter (below right).

Step 2e

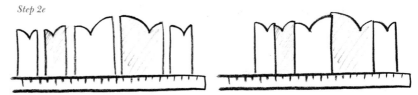

f. Trace the adjusted sculpted-hem pattern onto the paper and redraw any scalloped curves that might have lost their shape when adjusted. Cut out your new pattern.

3. Sew Your Sculpted Hem

a. Fold your additional outer-shell fabric right sides together, pin the sculpted-hem pattern to the fabric, and cut out two pieces. Be sure to transfer all dot markings—these will be your pivot points when sewing.

b. Take one hem piece and pin its short edges together; then sew at a ⅝" (16mm) seam allowance. Finish the seam edge with an over-edge zigzag stitch and press it open. Repeat with the second hem piece.

c. Line up your two hem pieces right sides together, matching up all scallops. Pin together, then sew at a ⅝" (16mm) seam allowance all the way around the scalloped edge, pivoting at the dot markings.

> **TIP:** *To pivot most efficiently at the dot markings, stop sewing, leave the needle in the fabric, lift the presser foot, and turn your work, remembering to realign your edge at ⅝" (16mm). Put your presser foot back down.*

d. Trim the seam allowance down to ¼" (6mm). Clip the curves and cut into the dot markings without clipping the stitches.

e. Turn your hem right side out and press, making sure that the curves of your sculpted hem are nice and round and that the valleys are crisp points.

4. Attach Your Sculpted Hem

a. The sculpted hem is going to add length, so now is the time to adjust your skirt-body length accordingly: Pin the hem to the bottom of your skirt and decide where you want it to hit. Once you find the perfect length, figure out how much shorter your skirt body should be; then subtract ⅝" (16mm) from this number. Trim that amount of fabric from the bottom of your skirt body.

EXAMPLE: We wanted our skirt body to be 5⅛" (13cm) shorter than the original length: 5⅛" (13cm) - ⅝" (16mm) = 4½" (11.5cm). We trimmed 4½" (11.5cm) from the bottom of our skirt.

b. Match up the cut edges of your scalloped hem with the right side of the bottom of your skirt, lining up the sculpted-hem seam with the left-side seam of your skirt.

c. Pin all four cut edges (outer shell, lining, and two hem layers) together. Sew a ⅝" (16mm) seam allowance all the way around. Finish the seam allowance edges together with an over-edge zigzag stitch and press it up toward the top of your skirt.

d. Topstitch ¼" (6mm) from the edge of this seam allowance to hold it in place.

e. Give your skirt a final pressing.

All in the Seams

Working curved inset seams and fanciful trims, like pom-poms,
rickrack, and piping, into a skirt is a great way to add interest.

Materials List

- ☐ Pencil pattern (pages 103–104)
- ☐ Basic sewing supplies
- ☐ 1½ yds (1.4m) main fabric
- ☐ 9" (23cm) invisible zipper
- ☐ 1 piece 22½" (57cm) long yarn; 1 piece 14" (35.5cm) long yarn (for creating curves)
- ☐ ½ yd (45.5cm) contrast fabric
- ☐ 1 yd (0.9m) decorative trim
- ☐ ½" (13mm) wide single-fold bias tape

FABRIC TIP: We used a patterned, medium-to-heavyweight cotton with a solid-colored, medium-weight four-ply silk for contrast. Four-ply silk is one of our favorite fabrics to sew with because it's stable yet luxurious; and it comes in some amazingly vibrant colors. Just remember: Whenever you add fabric to the bottom of a skirt, go lighter in weight for best results. Feel free to get creative when selecting your trim, but for this project you'll want to choose one that curves nicely.

1. Make Your Basic Skirt

Make a Pencil skirt following Steps 1–3 in Building Your Basic skirt (pages 16–17). Put the back piece to the side; you will be working with your skirt front for this project.

2. Make Your Curves

a. Lay your skirt front right side up. Starting at the bottom-right corner, measure 13½" (34cm) across the bottom of your skirt and pin down one end of the longer piece of yarn; now measure 13½" (34cm) up the right side of your skirt and pin down the other end of the longer piece of yarn.

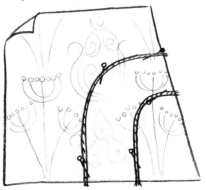

Steps 2a–c

b. Repeat with the shorter piece of yarn, but measure across and up only 8" (20cm).

c. Shape the yarn between the pins into nice curves. The curves should be situated 5½" (14cm) away from one another the entire distance.

d. Use tailor's chalk to sketch the curves alongside the yarn, then remove the yarn. These chalk lines are cutting lines.

e. Transfer your skirt's grain line to both curved pieces, which you're going to be cutting off to use as patterns: Fold the skirt front in half lengthwise, wrong sides together, creating a center-front fold. For the larger curve, measure 2" (5cm) over and 2" (5cm) up from the bottom of your skirt's fold; put a safety pin here, through the top layer only. Repeat twice more, measuring 2" (5cm) over from the fold and 2" (5cm) up from each safety pin (for a total of three safety pins). For the smaller curve, repeat this process, but measure 7" (18cm) over from the fold.

f. Unfold the fabric and cut the top chalk line; then cut the lower line. You now have your new pattern pieces.

g. Lay both of the pattern pieces right sides up on the right side of a single layer of contrast fabric, making sure the grain lines are parallel to the selvage edge.

h. Label your two pieces A (larger piece) and B (smaller piece).

i. On A, add a 1¼" (3cm) seam allowance to the top curved edge and a ⅝" (16mm) seam allowance to the bottom edge. Chalk the lines directly onto your contrast fabric.

j. Add ⅝" (16mm) seam allowance to only the top curved edge of B. Again, chalk the line directly onto the fabric.

k. Extend hem- and side-seam lines to meet the seam allowances; cut A and B out of your contrast fabric.

3. Attach Your Curves

a. Pin on your decorative trim, starting at the upper-right curved edge of both contrast pieces. Make sure the decorative edge of the trim is away from the cut edge.

b. Sew the trim on ⅝" (16mm) from the edge of the fabric with the zipper foot.

c. To attach A to B, pin the concave curve of A to the convex curve of B. It might seem as if one piece is much larger than the other, but start at the beginning, skip to the end, then ease in the rest. Don't worry, it will fit!

d. Using the zipper foot, sew next to the decorative part of the trim at a ⅝" (16mm) seam allowance, attaching the two layers. Sewing a curved seam can be tricky, but it will fit together.

e. Pin the convex curve of A to the concave curve of your skirt, right sides together, matching up the cut edges as you go. Start pinning at the top right corner of the curve.

Step 3e

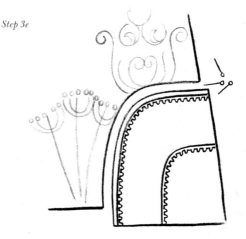

f. Sew the layers together as you did in Step 3d. Finish all seam edges together with an over-edge zigzag stitch, then press down.

4. Pin-Fit Your Skirt

Match up your skirt front and back, right sides together. Place safety pins every 3" (7.5cm) along the side seams at a ⅝" (16mm) seam allowance. Try on your skirt and make any adjustments.

5. Sew Your Side Seams

If you did not make any changes when pin-fitting, stitch the side seams at a ⅝" (16mm) seam allowance; if you adjusted the safety pins, chalk a vertical mark over each pin, then connect your vertical marks into a continuous line on both sides of your skirt. Sew along these new stitching lines, then trim the seam allowances to ⅝" (16mm). Finish the seam allowances.

6. Sew Your Darts

a. Match up the markings for the dart legs, one on top of the other with the right sides of the fabric together, creating a fold. Keep the fold on your right and the main part of the skirt on your left. Slide the two layers over each other until the dart-tip marking is on the fold. Securely pin the dart down. Repeat for all darts.

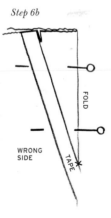

Step 6b

WRONG SIDE

FOLD

TAPE

b. Lay down a piece of basting tape that's slightly longer than the length of the dart so that the tape's right edge makes a straight line from the cut marks to the dart-tip marking. Sew right next to the tape, starting at the top of the dart where the cuts are, to the dart tip. Repeat for all darts. Press the dart fabric toward the center back of your skirt.

7. Sew Your Waistband

a. Measure the circumference of the top of your skirt and add 1¼" (3cm) for a seam allowance. Cut a piece of bias tape to this length.

b. Pin the bias tape right side up to the right side of the top of your skirt: open the zipper and extend one end of the bias tape ⅝" (16mm) past the zipper edge; continue pinning the bias tape around the skirt, covering the skirt's stay-stitching and also slightly overlapping the cut edge, until the tape extends ⅝" (16mm) past the other zipper edge. Sew closely to the bias tape's lower edge. Trim any threads and/or fabric extending past the bias tape no thinner than ⅜" (10mm).

c. Fold the extra bias tape on the ends toward the wrong side of the fabric; then fold the rest of the bias tape toward the wrong side of your skirt, far enough over so that you cannot see it from the outside. Pin the tape in place around your skirt. Sew closely to the bias tape's lower edge, starting and stopping your stitches about ¼" (6mm) from the zipper teeth. Turn your skirt inside out, and press the entire top of the skirt.

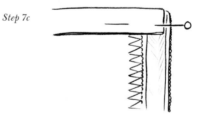

Step 7c

8. Finish Your Skirt

Hem your skirt with a 1" (2.5cm) hem allowance: fold the bottom-cut edge ½" (13mm), then fold ½" (13mm) again, hiding the raw edge; stitch. Press your skirt and do a final thread check.

VARIATION: Feel like a challenge? Curve your back piece, too, and match the front and back half circles at your side seams.

Tie Me Up

Add an element of surprise to the back of this skirt by replacing the zipper with a corset closure.

Materials List

- ☐ Pencil pattern (pages 103-104)
- ☐ Basic sewing supplies
- ☐ 1½ yds (1.4m) main fabric
- ☐ ½" (13mm) wide single-fold bias tape
- ☐ Placket 1 and 2 patterns (pages 118-119)
- ☐ ⅜ yd (35cm) contrast fabric
- ☐ ⅜ yd (35cm) fusible interfacing
- ☐ 12 size #0 (¼", or 6mm) grommets
- ☐ Grommet pliers (to set in grommets)
- ☐ 2 yds (1.8m) cording

FABRIC TIP: We used a plaid taffeta for the skirt body and a solid-colored four-ply silk for the placket. Taffeta has a certain stiffness that looks great on dressy styles; the four-ply silk is easy to work with yet also contributes to the classic party-dress formality of this skirt.

1. Make Your Basic Skirt

a. Make a Pencil skirt following Steps 1–2 in Building Your Basic Skirt (pages 16–17).

b. Skip to Steps 4–6 (pages 18–20), with one exception: during your pin-fit, pin your back seam together instead of sewing it.

c. Finish the edges of both center-back seams with an over-edge zigzag stitch.

d. Pin the seams right sides together; then measure down 10" (25cm) from the top of your skirt and sew the center-back seam closed from that point to the bottom. Press the seam allowance open, not only where you sewed but also above the stitching, where the center-back seam is open.

e. Topstitch ½" (13mm) from the edge of the opening to keep the seam allowance in place. Stitch down the right side of the opening, pivot across the bottom, then stitch back up the left side.

2. Sew Your Waistband

a. Measure the circumference of the top of your skirt and cut a piece of bias tape this length (do not add seam allowance).

b. Pin the bias tape right side up to the right side of the top of your skirt: Match up one end of the bias tape with the back-center edge; continue pinning the bias tape around the skirt, covering the skirt's stay-stitching and also slightly over-lapping the top-cut edge, until the tape is even with the other back-center edge. Sew closely to the bias tape's lower edge. Trim any threads and/or fabric extending past the bias tape no thinner than ⅜" (10mm).

c. Fold the bias tape toward the wrong side of your skirt, far enough over so that you cannot see it from the outside. Pin the tape in place around your skirt. Sew closely to the bias tape's lower edge. Turn your skirt inside out, and press the entire top of the skirt.

3. Create Your Placket

a. Align the register marks (the circles) of the two placket patterns and tape them together.

b. Cut eight plackets: four from your contrast fabric and four from interfacing. Transfer all markings from the pattern to your fabric.

NOTE: Both pairs of placket pieces cut from your contrast fabric need to be mirror images of each other. Fold your fabric right sides together, then cut through both layers to achieve this.

c. For the placket flap (this piece is sewn behind the corset closure to eliminate gaps), make a rectangle measuring 5½" by 10½" (14cm by 26.5cm). Cut one flap out of contrast fabric and one out of interfacing.

d. Fuse the interfacing to the wrong sides of the fabric for all five fabric pieces (four placket pieces and one placket flap).

e. Place one pair of placket pieces right sides together. Sew a ⅝" (16mm) seam allowance from the dot marking on the center seam to the bottom of the placket pair.

Step 3e

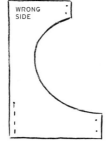

f. Repeat on the second pair of placket pieces. Press the seam allowances open.

g. Place both placket pieces right sides together and sew together across the top edge and down the center back on the left side, stopping at the existing line of stitches. Repeat on the right side.

Step 3g

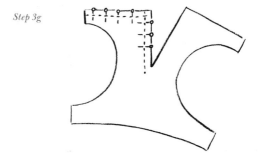

NOTE: Be careful not to catch any extra layers in the sewn seam near the bottom of the center back.

h. Clip excess fabric from the corners and trim the seam allowances to ¼" (6mm) to reduce bulk. Turn right sides out and press the layers flat.

NOTE: Make sure you have a nice sharp corner at the top center on both sides of the placket; when closed, the top corners should be even with each other.

i. Stitch the curves just shy of ⅝" (16mm); these stitches will be the guide for clipping and folding under the seam allowance.

NOTE: Sew this line of stitching for each layer individually; at this point, your two placket pieces should only be stitched together where you stitched in Step 3g.

j. Once you have the line of stitching, clip your curves every ¾" (2cm), then fold toward the wrong side and press. Make sure your curves are even and crisp, with the raw edges hidden to the wrong side. From this point on we are going to refer to the two sides as "placket" and "placket lining," even though both sides are identical.

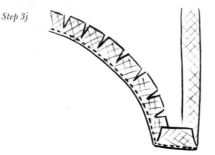

Step 3j

NOTE: All four sides should be the same size and shape.

k. Fold the placket flap in half lenthwise, right sides together. Sew both short ends at a ⅝" (16mm) seam allowance. Clip excess fabric from the corners, turn right side out, and press.

l. The placket flap will be sewn to the left side of the placket lining: Place the raw edges of the placket flap ¾" (2cm) from and parallel to the finished center-back edge of the placket lining; stitch ⅛" (3mm) away from the raw edges through only the flap and lining layer. Fold the flap at the stitch line toward the center back and sew ¼" (6mm) from the fold.

4. Attach Your Placket

a. Before sewing the skirt and placket together, you need to sandwich the back corners of your skirt between the two layers of the placket: Using a hand-sewing needle and thread, tie a knot in the end of your thread and stick the needle in the skirt fabric at the top corner of your center-back seam. Now stick the needle through the placket from the inside, pull the thread tight, bringing the piece of fabric into the corner of the placket. Tie off the thread so that the fabric stays in place. Repeat for the other top corner of your center-back seam.

b. Starting at the top edge of your placket, pin the placket to the skirt through all three layers (placket, skirt, and placket lining). Make sure the placket is as even with the top of the skirt as possible. Pin all the way around the placket.

c. Sew around the side and bottom ⅛" (3mm) from the placket's edge, making sure all three layers are caught in the stitches.

NOTE: If you miss the lining at any point, hand-sew those areas from the inside of your skirt.

d. Transfer the grommet-location markings from the pattern to your placket, and set in your grommets at those markings.

TIP: *Practice placing grommets on a scrap of fabric before cutting holes in your skirt.*

e. Lace your skirt through the grommets from top to bottom with the cording.

5. Finish Your Skirt

Hem your skirt with a 1" (2.5cm) hem allowance: fold the bottom-cut edge ½" (13mm), then fold ½" (13mm) again, hiding the raw edge; stitch. Press your skirt and do a final thread check.

Sculpt Me, Shape Me

Using pleating, this project adds a unique and textured detail
to the front of your skirt and an incredibly cool asymmetrical hem.

Materials List

☐ Pencil pattern (pages 103-104)

☐ Basic sewing supplies

☐ 1½ yds (1.4m) fabric + ½ yd (45.5cm) additional fabric

☐ 9" (23cm) invisible zipper

☐ ½" (13mm) wide single-fold bias tape

FABRIC TIP: We used a textured, light- to medium-weight acetate fabric. This skirt is about the addition of texture through horizontal pleats so starting with textured fabric just adds to its overall interest.

1. Make Your Basic Skirt

The layout of and cutting instructions for your skirt front are explained here, because the process is different from the one described in Building Your Basic Skirt.

a. Fold the wrong sides of your fabric together, creating a fold parallel to the selvage edge.

b. Lay the skirt-front pattern piece on your fabric, placing the center front on the fold of your fabric and leaving at least 13" (33cm) of fabric below the pattern piece. Cut along the top and side of the pattern, not the bottom edge.

c. Before unpinning the pattern piece, chalk a line 13" (33cm) from the existing bottom. Open the fabric so that you are looking at the entire skirt front with the right side facing you.

d. For the skirt back, follow Steps 1–3 in Building Your Basic Skirt (pages 16–17).

2. Make Your New Skirt-Front Bottom

a. Measure up 1" (2.5cm) from the pattern hemline on the right side of the skirt front and make a chalk mark. Now measure the distance across the front of the skirt at the pattern hemline; refer to this measurement as A.

b. Using the distance of measurement A, chalk a line from the mark you made on the right side to where you connect to your line, 13" (33cm) away from the bottom of the skirt.

NOTE: Since you marked the 13" (33cm) line while the fabric was folded, extend the line the distance of the bottom of the fabric, if needed.

c. For the other side of your skirt bottom, start your measurment from where the first line intersects the bottom line. Measure up 22" (56cm) and make a mark on the left-side seam; chalk that line in.

Steps 2a–c

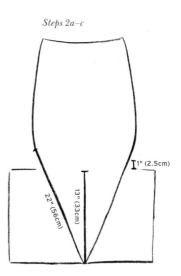

22" (56cm)

13" (33cm)

1" (2.5cm)

d. These two chalk lines are your new skirt bottom; cut out your fabric on these lines.

e. Fold your skirt front in half lengthwise and place a pin at the center top (to remind yourself where the center is), then unfold it. Stay-stitch ⅜" (10mm) away from the top-cut edge: start at the left edge and sew to the center, stop, flip over your skirt front, and stay-stitch from the non-sewn edge to the center.

3. Make Your Pleats

a. Starting at the bottom of your skirt front, chalk a mark up the left side of the angle every 1" (2.5cm) for 22" (56cm). You should have twenty-two marks.

> **TIP:** *Make the marks small enough to hide in the seam allowance.*

b. To fold the first pleat, count up from the bottom to the 6th mark, then fold the fabric down to the 4th mark; this creates a pleat that is 1" (2.5cm) wide.

NOTE: Each pleat will be the same size.

c. For the next pleat, count up to the 9th mark and fold down to the 7th mark; then count up to the 12th mark and fold down to the 10th mark for the third pleat. Continue counting up three marks and folding down two marks until you have six pleats.

d. Baste the pleats ⅜" (10mm) from the left-cut edge.

4. Stitch Your Pleats

Stitch each pleat ⅛" (3mm) from the lower edge where the fold is, increasing the stitching length by ½" (13mm) for each pleat: sew the topmost pleat 2" (5cm) from the left edge and the bottommost pleat 4½" (11.5cm) from the left edge.

Step 4

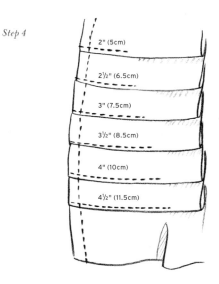

2" (5cm)
2½" (6.5cm)
3" (7.5cm)
3½" (8.5cm)
4" (10cm)
4½" (11.5cm)

NOTE: This pleating technique creates an asymmetrical hem that appears straight when you walk.

5. Hem Your Skirt

Before sewing the side seams, hem the skirt's front and back pieces separately: sew a 1" (2.5cm) hem allowance on both the front and back pieces.

NOTE: Because the front hem is angled and the back hem is straight, hemming the pieces separately will make it easier to join them together at the side seams.

> **TIP:** *For this project, we made a blind hem because our fabric had a lot of texture we didn't want to flatten with a straight stitch. Most machines have a blind hem foot, but if yours doesn't, sew a regular hem.*

6. Sew a Gathering Stitch

On your skirt front, run a gathering stitch—using the longest stitch length on your machine—$3/8$" (10mm) from the left-cut edge, starting from the bottom of the lowest pleat to the hem; this will help you ease the skirt front into the skirt back when pin-fitting.

Step 6

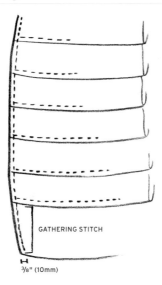

GATHERING STITCH

$3/8$" (10mm)

7. Pin-Fit Your Skirt

a. Match up your skirt front and back, right sides together. Place safety pins every 3" (7.5 cm) along the side seams at a $5/8$" (16mm) seam allowance. Try on your skirt and make any adjustments.

b. The pleated-side seam may require a small amount of easing in to match it up, so use the gathering stitch you sewed in Step 6: grab hold of one end of the gathering stitch and slide the pleated edge up and down to achieve a nice even look. Your pieces should match up $5/8$" (16mm) from the edge.

NOTE: When gathering fabric, make sure you don't lose the other end of the thread (hold tight!) or break the thread (be gentle).

8. Sew Your Side Seams

a. If you did not make any changes when pin-fitting, stitch the side seams at a $5/8$" (16mm) seam allowance; if you adjusted the safety pins, chalk a vertical mark over each pin, then connect your vertical marks into a continuous line on both sides of your skirt. Sew along these new stitching lines, then trim the seam allowances to $5/8$" (16mm).

b. Trim the extra bit of fabric hanging over the pleated edge, then finish the seam allowances and press toward the back of your skirt. Tack your seam allowance down at the hem, with a few hand-sewn stitches, for a clean look.

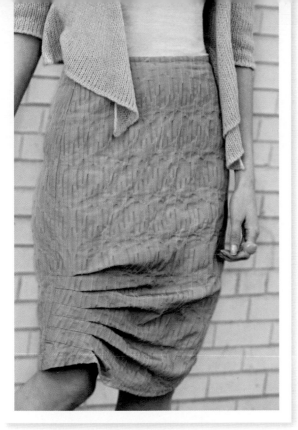

10. Sew Your Waistband

a. Measure the circumference of the top of your skirt and add 1¼" (3cm) for a seam allowance. Cut a piece of bias tape to this length.

b. Pin the bias tape right side up to the right side of the top of your skirt: open the zipper and extend one end of the bias tape ⅝" (16mm) past the zipper edge; continue pinning the bias tape around the skirt, covering the skirt's stay-stitching and also slightly overlapping the cut edge, until the tape extends ⅝" (16mm) past the other zipper edge. Sew closely to the bias tape's lower edge. Trim any threads and/or fabric extending past the bias tape no thinner than ⅜" (10mm).

c. Fold the extra bias tape on the ends toward the wrong side of the fabric; then fold the rest of the bias tape toward the wrong side of your skirt, far enough over so that you cannot see it from the outside. Pin the tape in place around your skirt. Sew closely to the bias tape's lower edge, starting and stopping your stitches about ¼" (6mm) from the zipper teeth. Turn your skirt inside out, and press the entire top of the skirt.

Step 10c

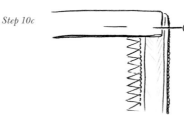

11. Finish Your Skirt

Press your skirt and do a final thread check.

9. Sew Your Darts

a. Match up the markings for the dart legs, one on top of the other with the right sides of the fabric together, creating a fold. Keep the fold on your right and the main part of the skirt on your left. Slide the two layers over each other until the dart-tip marking is on the fold. Securely pin the dart down. Repeat for all darts.

Step 9b

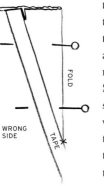

WRONG
SIDE

FOLD

TAPE

b. Lay down a piece of basting tape that's slightly longer than the length of the dart so that the tape's right edge makes a straight line from the cut marks to the dart-tip marking. Sew right next to the tape, starting at the top of the dart where the cuts are, to the dart tip. Repeat for all darts. Press the dart fabric toward the center back of your skirt.

Baby Got Bustle Back

This flirty, fitted skirt with an eye-popping bustle at the back begs to be paired with sexy, seamed stockings!

Materials List

- ☐ Pencil pattern (pages 103-104)
- ☐ Basic sewing supplies
- ☐ 1½ yds (1.4m) main fabric + ½ yd (45.5cm) additional fabric
- ☐ 9" (23cm) invisible zipper
- ☐ ½" (13mm) wide single-fold bias tape
- ☐ ⅜ yd (35cm) polka-dot flocked tulle (in contrasting color)

FABRIC TIP: We used solid-colored, wool suiting for the skirt with dotted flocked tulle for embellishment on the ruffles. We like the contradiction of a conservative fabric paired with a whimsical accent.

1. Make Your Basic Skirt

Complete a Pencil skirt following all of the instructions in Building Your Basic Skirt (pages 16–22).

VARIATION: Attaching a bustle is a great way to upgrade a skirt you already have hanging in your closet.

2. Make Your Ruffles

a. To make your ruffles, cut four rectangles from the additional main fabric in these dimensions:

- ☻ 11¼" x 5" (28.5cm x 12.5cm)
- ☻ 13¼" x 5" (33.5cm x 12.5cm)
- ☻ 15¼" x 5" (38.5cm x 12.5cm)
- ☻ 17¼" x 5" (43.5cm x 12.5cm)

And four rectangles from the tulle in these dimensions:

- ☻ 11¼" x 5⅜" (28.5cm x 13.5cm)
- ☻ 13¼" x 5⅜" (33.5cm x 13.5cm)
- ☻ 15¼" x 5⅜" (38.5cm x 13.5cm)
- ☻ 17¼" x 5⅜" (43.5cm x 13.5cm)

b. Sew a ½" (13mm) hem at the bottom (one of the long sides) of all four of your fabric pieces: fold the fabric ¼" (6mm) twice toward the wrong side and stitch in place; press.

c. Line up the fabric pieces with their corresponding-sized tulle pieces, right sides together, with the tulle extending approximately 1" (2.5cm) past the hemmed edge of the fabric pieces.

d. With a ⅝" (16mm) seam allowance, sew both layers together along the top and sides (not the hemmed edge), pivoting when you get ⅝" (16mm) from each corner.

e. Clip the top corners and trim the two tulle edges that extend beyond the fabric hem so that they're even with the stitching lines.

f. Finish all raw edges with an over-edge zigzag stitch where the two fabrics are sewn together.

Step 2e

g. Turn your ruffles right sides out and press flat.

> **TIP:** *Many tulle fabrics can be sensitive to heat, so test a scrap for the proper iron setting before pressing.*

h. At the right and left corners of each ruffle, sew the fabric to the tulle: topstitch six stitches forward, reverse back over these stitches, and sew six stitches forward again over your hem so that they blend right in.

i. Using the longest stitch length on your machine, run a gathering stitch $3/8$" (10mm) away from the top edge of your ruffles. Do not lockstitch.

j. To gather each ruffle, hold one of the gathering stitch ends, and slide the fabric over the thread, gathering the fabric as you go.

NOTE: When gathering fabric, make sure you don't lose the other end of the thread (hold tight!) or break the thread (be gentle).

3. Attach Your Ruffles

a. Position the ruffles on the back of your skirt, moving from bottom to top (largest ruffle to smallest ruffle). The fabric of the bottommost ruffle should be even with the hemline, with the tulle extending 1" (2.5cm) past the hem. The fabric of each successive ruffle should end at the top of the ruffle beneath it, with the tulle similarly extending 1" (2.5cm) below the fabric.

NOTE: The top ruffle should be below the zipper of your skirt.

b. Starting with the topmost ruffle (the smallest one) locate the ruffle's center on its gathered edge, then place the ruffle on your skirt, centered over the center-back seam and extending $2½$" (6.5cm) on either side for a total width of 5" (12.5cm). Pin the ruffle in place, evenly gathering the fabric.

Step 3b

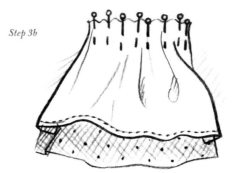

c. Repeat with the three remaining ruffles: the second ruffle should extend $3½$" (9cm) over either side of the center-back seam; the third ruffle, $4½$" (11.5cm); and the fourth (bottommost) ruffle, $5½$" (14cm).

NOTE: When pinned straight across their tops, the ruffles flare out at their bottoms.

d. Sew each ruffle onto your skirt $1/8$" (3mm) from the top of the ruffle; this stitching line will be above your gathering stitch.

e. Once the ruffles are sewn, remove the gathering stitches.

> **TIP:** *If you're finding it difficult to sew over the gathers, use a tool like a stiletto or any other small, pointy object to help you evenly (and gently) push your gathers under the presser foot.*

Flare

On the Flip Side

This alternative to traditional appliqué technique leaves raw edges, giving your skirt a handmade, one-of-a-kind feel.

Materials List

- ☐ Flare pattern (pages 105–107)
- ☐ Basic sewing supplies
- ☐ 1½ yds (1.4m) main fabric
- ☐ 9" (23cm) invisible zipper
- ☐ ⅜ yd (35cm) contrast fabric
- ☐ ¼ yd (23cm) 45" (114cm) wide fusible interfacing
- ☐ Button

FABRIC TIP: We chose a patterned, medium-weight cotton for the main skirt and a solid-colored, medium-weight cotton with texture (lace) for the contrast. Look for two cottons or cotton blends that are similar in weight but different in color and texture, so your appliqués really pop.

1. Make Your Basic Skirt

Make a Flare skirt following Steps 1–3 in Building Your Basic Skirt (pages 16–17).

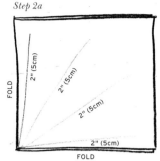

Step 2a

2. Make Your Circles

a. Create three circle patterns: fold a piece of paper in quarters, then measure and mark the radius of each circle. The small circle's radius is 2" (5cm), the medium circle's radius is 3" (7.5cm), and the large circle's radius is 4" (10cm).

b. Connect the radius lines and cut out each circle pattern; unfold the paper. Using these pattern pieces, cut out three large, four medium, and five small circles from your contrast fabric.

3. Practice Sewing an Appliqué

When attempting a new technique, it's important to do a practice run to make sure you are comfortable with the process before applying it to your skirt. To practice, you'll need one small fabric circle and a scrap of fabric approximately 6" by 6" (15cm by 15cm).

a. Finish the edge of the circle with an over-edge zigzag stitch.

> **TIP:** *If the circle seems to be fraying more than you like, sew a second zigzag stitch ¼" (6mm) in from the first line of stitching.*

b. Lay the circle on your fabric scrap, with the right side of the circle facing the wrong side of the scrap; pin in place, making sure the circle is lying completely flat.

c. With the wrong side of the circle facing you, stitch ⅜" (10mm) from the edge of your circle all the way around, lockstitching when you start and stop. Stitch a second line ⅝" (16mm) from the circle's edge; this creates an interesting double-stitch detail.

d. With the right side of the fabric scrap facing up, pull the fabric scrap away from the fabric circle. Make a small snip, being careful to cut only into the top (fabric scrap) layer. Insert the bottom blade of your scissors into the snipped hole and, slowly and accurately, cut ⅛" (3mm) from your stitches. As you cut out the top layer, your contrast fabric will start to show through.

Step 3d

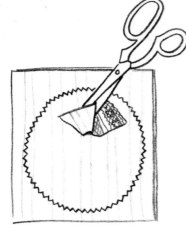

e. Cut all the way around the circle.

f. Once you feel comfortable with this process and are happy with the results, move on to your skirt.

> **TIP:** *The remaining ⅛" (3mm) of fabric surrounding your contrast circle may fray over time; this is part of the technique. If you prefer a cleaner look, sew an over-edge zigzag stitch with a shorter stitch length where the main fabric meets the contrast fabric.*

4. Sew Your Appliqués

Place the fabric circles on your skirt, then sew and cut them following Steps 3a–e. Follow our circle placement or situate the circles wherever you like.

> **TIP:** *If you have a sheer contrast fabric like ours, don't place the circles too high up on the skirt—or you might stop traffic walking down the street!*

Step 4

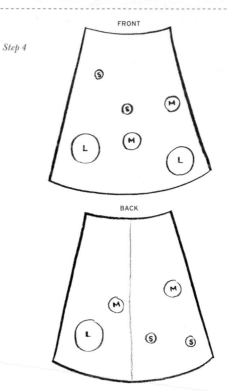

> **TIP:** *For even more detail, thread your machine with a bright, contrasting color.*

5. Pin-Fit Your Skirt

Match up your skirt front and back, right sides together. Place safety pins every 3" (7.5 cm) along the side seams at a ⅝" (16mm) seam allowance. Try your skirt on and make any adjustments.

6. Sew Your Side Seams

If you did not make any changes when pin-fitting, stitch the side seams at a ⅝" (16mm) seam allowance; if you adjusted the safety pins, chalk a vertical mark over each pin, then connect your vertical marks into a continuous line on both sides of your skirt. Sew along these new stitching lines, then trim the seam allowanaces to ⅝" (16mm). Finish the seam allowances.

7. Sew Your Waistband

a. Fuse the interfacing to the wrong side of your waistband. With the edge of the waistband even with the top-cut edge of the skirt, right sides together, overlap your waistband ⅝" (16mm) past the right zipper edge. Pin both layers together until you reach the other side of the zipper. Sew a ⅝" (16mm) seam allowance all the way around the top of your skirt, starting and stopping at the zipper. Trim the left edge of the waistband down to 1⅞" (4.5cm), if necessary.

b. Fold your waistband in half, right sides together. On the right-back side, sew the edge of the waistband at a ⅝" (16mm) seam allowance, stopping ⅝" (16mm) from the bottom corner. On the left-back side, sew the edge at a ⅝" (16mm) seam allowance; pivot ⅝" (16mm) from the bottom corner, then continue sewing 1¼" (3cm). Clip the corners and press the seam allowance up toward the waistband. Turn the waistband right side out and poke out the corners of the tabs.

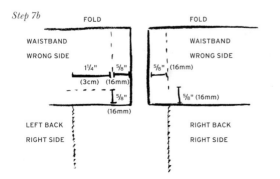

Step 7b

c. Fold the waistband's unattached edge under ⅜" (10mm) on the inside of your skirt so that the fold hangs a bit lower than the existing seam. Pin, then sew the seam allowance with the zipper foot on the right side of your skirt in the "ditch" created by the existing seam, making sure that you catch the fabric on the other side.

d. Press the waistband, then make a buttonhole—one that corresponds to the size of your button—in the left-side tab. Sew your button onto the right side of the waistband.

8. Finish Your Skirt

Hem your skirt with a 1" (2.5cm) hem allowance: fold the bottom-cut edge ½" (13mm), then fold ½" (13mm) again, hiding the raw edge; stitch. Press your skirt and do a final thread check.

VARIATION: This is a great technique to try on an existing skirt that needs an update.

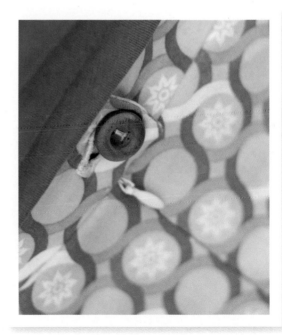

Summer in the City

Nothing says chic like an ankle-length skirt. Bold yet refined, this conversation piece will take you to any summer cocktail party in style.

Materials List

- ☐ Flare pattern (pages 105–107)
- ☐ Basic sewing supplies
- ☐ 4½ yds (2.7m) fabric

NOTE: This is the maximum amount of fabric to buy. If you want to buy the amount of fabric for your size, double the amount of fabric on the Flare skirt chart (page 14) for your size and fabric width.

- ☐ 9" (23cm) invisible zipper
- ☐ ¼ yd (23cm) 45" (1.2m) fusible interfacing
- ☐ Button

FABRIC TIP: We used a patterned, lightweight, opaque silk; a polyester or rayon print will also work. Look for a fabric that is bold, colorful, and drapey. Make sure your choice is opaque enough so that it doesn't need to be lined.

1. Lay Out Your Fabric

The layout of and cutting instructions for this skirt are explained here, because the process is different from the one in Building Your Basic Skirt.

a. Fold your fabric with the selvage edges and right sides together. Lay the back pattern piece on the fabric, making sure to match up the grain line; pin in place.

> **TIP:** *Working with a lightweight fabric can be slippery, so pin the layers together at a few different points before pinning on the pattern to prevent it from sliding too much.*

b. Determine the desired length of your skirt: hold one end of a measuring tape at the point on your body where you want your skirt to sit (waistline, hips, or in-between), then measure down to where you want it to end. Measure from the backside of your body, which will give you the longest distance to the floor. Add $1\frac{5}{8}$" (4cm) to your measurement.

c. At center back, measure down this amount from the top of the back pattern piece and make a chalk mark. Now measure the distance from the bottom of the pattern piece to your chalk mark; call this measurement A. Measurement A will determine the new hemline for your back and front pieces.

d. To create a new curved hemline on your skirt back, make a chalk mark every 1½" (3.8cm) the distance of measurement A below the pattern hemline; then chalk a straight line to connect the existing side seams to the new hemline.

e. Repeat this process for the skirt front: lay the pattern piece on the fold, pin in place, and chalk in the new hemline.

NOTE: To ensure that you have enough fabric for your skirt, make sure to lay out and add the new hemlines to both pieces before cutting.

f. Place your waistband pattern piece on your fabric as shown in the layout diagram on page 16; cut one waistband piece out of fabric and one out of interfacing.

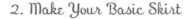

2. Make Your Basic Skirt

Return to Step 1b in Building Your Basic Skirt (page 16) and continue to the end to complete Summer in the City.

NOTE: Though your pieces are longer, the construction is the same as the basic Flare skirt.

Tips on Sewing Silk

Here are a few tips to keep in mind when sewing slippery silk:

- Use a sharp sewing-machine needle. Silk snags easily, so if you notice any little pulls in the fabric, change your needle.

- Use sharp pins. If your fabric seems to be resisting a pin, don't force it; try a different pin. If you sew with silk often, buy silk pins made specifically for this type of fabric; they are very thin and sharp.

- Practice with fabric scraps. To get the hang of sewing a slippery seam, practicing first is always helpful and just might prevent frustration later.

Put It in Print

This project is our take on textile design using a stencil technique.
When it comes to choosing the color of your fabric paint, have fun!

Materials List

- ☐ Flare pattern (pages 105–107)
- ☐ Basic sewing supplies
- ☐ 2¼ yds (2m) fabric
- ☐ 9" (23cm) invisible zipper
- ☐ Stencil template (page 109)
- ☐ 2 acetate sheets
- ☐ Thin marker
- ☐ Hole punch
- ☐ Fabric paint
- ☐ Small paper plate (for your paint)
- ☐ Kitchen sponge (cut into 4 pieces)
- ☐ ¼ yd (23cm) 45" (114cm) wide fusible interfacing
- ☐ Button

FABRIC TIP: We used a solid-colored, medium-weight cotton shirting. This project is all about the print, so you want a stable fabric that won't shift while you're pinning the stencil to it.

1. Make Your Basic Skirt

Make a Flare skirt following Steps 1–3 in Building Your Basic Skirt (pages 16–17).

2. Make Your Stencil

a. Lay the template for this project beneath a sheet of acetate. With the marker, trace the lines of the image onto the plastic. Repeat with the second piece of acetate.

NOTE: You need two stencils because the design is a mirror image.

TIP: *If you are planning on making your skirt shorter or longer, photocopy the template at a smaller or larger size accordingly.*

b. Cut out all of the areas inside the marker lines.

NOTE: On the template, there are two small areas surrounded by lighter lines. Do not cut inside these lines; they stabilize the stencil. You'll fill in these areas with paint later.

c. Lay the two stencils on your work surface, so you have a mirror image. With your marker, label the stencils "right" and "left" to keep them straight.

Step 2d

d. With the hole punch, punch two holes 1" (2.5cm) away from each other in the upper-left and lower-right corners of the left stencil and the upper-right and lower-left corners of the right stencil; your pins will go through these holes.

3. Print Your Skirt

a. Lay your skirt front right side up, with the left side lengthwise and closest to you. Pin the stencil in place at the holes made in Step 2d. Lay the right stencil next to the left one with ⅝" (16mm) between them, so they are a mirror image of one another; then position the bottommost part of each stencil 1¼" (3cm) from your skirt's side seam.

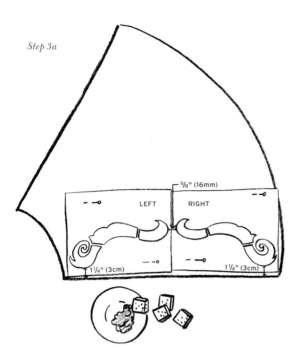

Step 3a

⁵⁄₈" (16mm)

LEFT   RIGHT

1¼" (3cm)   1¼" (3cm)

NOTE: Place the stencils equidistantly between the top and bottom of your skirt, accounting for a ⁵⁄₈" (16mm) waist allowance and a 1" (2.5cm) hem allowance.

b. Put some paint on the paper plate and make sure your sponge is soft; dampen it if necessary. With a small amount of paint on the sponge, use a dabbing technique to slowly fill in all open areas of the stencil.

> **TIP:** *For more control, dab with the smaller edge of your sponge.*

NOTE: Make sure you are completely happy with how the paint looks before removing the stencil. To avoid smearing the paint, remove the stencil by lifting it straight up from the fabric.

c. Cut one of the sponge pieces in half again, so you have a smaller sponge. Fill in the small, unpainted area that acted as the stencil stabilizer (see Step 2b) to complete the design.

Printing Tips

- Cover your work space with a plastic trash bag to protect it from paint spillage.

- Print your skirt and allow it to dry completely before sewing the side seams; it's very difficult to paint on fabric that is not lying flat.

- Practice painting on a fabric scrap before applying paint to your skirt.

> **TIP:** *Wipe down your stencil before reusing. Also, clean up any paint spills on your work surface at this point.*

d. Repeat Steps 3a–c on the right side of your skirt front.

e. Set your skirt front aside to dry completely before sewing. Follow the paint manufacturer's suggested drying time; heat-set if instructed.

> **TIP:** *If you're unsure of how long it will take for the paint to set, let your skirt front dry overnight.*

4. Pin-Fit Your Skirt

Match up your skirt front and back, right sides together. Place safety pins every 3" (7.5 cm) along the side seams at a $\frac{5}{8}$" (16mm) seam allowance. Make any adjustments.

5. Sew Your Side Seams

If you did not make any changes when pin-fitting, stitch the side seams at a $\frac{5}{8}$" (16mm) seam allowance; if you adjusted the safety pins, chalk a vertical mark over each pin, then connect your vertical marks into a continuous line on both sides of your skirt. Sew along these new stitching lines, then trim the seam allowances to $\frac{5}{8}$" (16mm). Finish the seam allowances.

6. Sew Your Waistband

a. Fuse the interfacing to the wrong side of your waistband. With the edge of the waistband even with the top-cut edge of the skirt, right sides together, overlap your waistband $\frac{5}{8}$" (16mm) past the right zipper edge. Pin both layers together until you reach the other side of the zipper. Sew a $\frac{5}{8}$" (16mm) seam allowance all the way around the top of your skirt, starting and stopping at the zipper. Trim the left edge of the waistband down to $1\frac{7}{8}$" (4.5cm), if necessary.

b. Fold your waistband in half, right sides together. On the right-back side, sew the edge of the waistband at a $\frac{5}{8}$" (16mm) seam allowance, stopping $\frac{5}{8}$" (16mm) from the bottom corner. On the left-back side, sew the edge at a $\frac{5}{8}$" (16mm) seam allowance; pivot $\frac{5}{8}$" (16mm) from the bottom corner, then continue sewing $1\frac{1}{4}$" (3cm). Clip the corners and press the seam allowance up toward the waistband. Turn the waistband right side out and poke out the corners of the tabs.

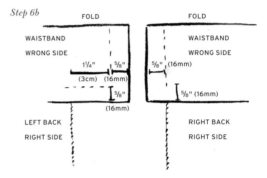

c. Fold the waistband's unattached edge under $\frac{3}{8}$" (10mm) on the inside of your skirt so that the fold hangs a bit lower than the existing seam. Pin, then sew the seam allowance with the zipper foot on the right side of your skirt in the "ditch" created by the existing seam, making sure that you catch the fabric on the other side.

d. Press the waistband, then make a buttonhole—one that corresponds to the size of your button—in the left-side tab. Sew your button onto the right side of the waistband.

7. Finish Your Skirt

Hem your skirt with a 1" (2.5cm) hem allowance: fold the bottom-cut edge $\frac{1}{2}$" (13mm), then fold $\frac{1}{2}$" (13mm) again, hiding the raw edge; stitch. Press your skirt and do a final thread check.

Take It Up a Notch

By widening the waistband and adding a button detail to this skirt, you'll create a sophisticated, high-waisted look.

Materials List

- ☐ Flare pattern
  (pages 105–107)

- ☐ Basic sewing supplies

- ☐ 2¼ yds (2m) main fabric
  + ¼ yd (23cm) additional
  fabric

- ☐ 9" (23cm) invisible zipper

- ☐ Paper

- ☐ Sculpted-waistband template
  (page 119)

- ☐ ¼ yd (23cm) lining fabric
  (for waistband)

- ☐ ¼ yd (23cm) 45" (114cm)
  wide fusible interfacing

- ☐ 9 medium-sized buttons

FABRIC TIP: We used a pin-
striped, cotton suiting and
a solid-colored, polyester
lining. Find a fabric that
reads tailored suit to give
the skirt the right feel. If you
prefer a more casual look,
choose a lightweight denim.

1. Make Your Basic Skirt

Make a Flare skirt following Step 1a in Building Your Basic Skirt
(page 16), omitting the waistband piece, then continue with Steps 1b–5
(pages 16–19).

2. Make Your Waistband

a. Measure the length of the original Flare waistband pattern for your
size (you do not need the pattern piece, just the measurement); call this
measurement A.

b. To make your new waistband pattern, you need a piece of paper that
is at least 6" (15cm) wide by the length of measurement A. (If you don't
have paper long enough to accommodate the pattern, tape a few pieces
together.) Lay the sculpted-waistband template slightly left of center. To
sketch the rest of the waistband, extend the left side, from the center of
the sculpted-waistband template, the length of measurement A *minus* ⅝"
(16mm); extend the right side, from the center of the sculpted-waistband
template, the length of measurement A *plus* ⅝" (16mm).

EXAMPLE: Our measurement A was 38½" (98cm): 38½" (98cm) –
⅝" (16mm) = 37⅞" (96cm)—the length to extend the left side of the
waistband from the center of the sculpted-waistband template. 38½"
(98cm) + ⅝" (16mm) = 39⅛" (99.5cm)—the length to extend the right
side of the waistband from the center of the sculpted-waistband template.

c. Cut one new waistband out of main fabric, one out of lining fabric,
and one out of fusible interfacing (shiny side up).

NOTE: When cutting out the lining fabric, place the pattern wrong side
up on the fabric—the lining is the reverse of the skirt fabric.

d. Fuse the interfacing to the skirt fabric.

e. Pin the two waistband pieces right sides together. Sew along the top,
curved edge, starting and stopping ⅝" (16mm) from the sides.

f. Clip the curved edge so that the waistband lies flat around the
sculpted area.

Step 2f

3. Sew Your Waistband

a. Locate the centers of the waistband and skirt front and match up their cut edges; pin right sides together. On your skirt back, overlap your waistband ⅝" (16mm) past the right zipper edge, with the edge of the waistband even with the top-cut edge of the skirt, right sides together. Pin both layers together until you reach the other side of the zipper, where the waistband extends 1⅞" (4.5cm). Sew a ⅝" (16mm) seam allowance all the way around the top of your skirt, starting and stopping at the zipper.

b. Fold your waistband in half, right sides together. On the right-back side, sew the edge of the waistband at a ⅝" (16mm) seam allowance, stopping ⅝" (16mm) from the bottom corner. On the left-back side, sew the edge at a ⅝" (16mm) seam allowance; pivot ⅝" (16mm) from the bottom corner, then continue sewing 1¼" (3cm). Clip the corners and press the seam allowance up toward the waistband. Turn the waistband right side out and poke out the corners of the tabs.

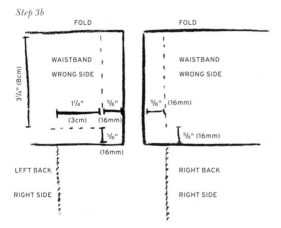

Step 3b

FOLD   FOLD

WAISTBAND   WAISTBAND
WRONG SIDE   WRONG SIDE

3¼" (8cm)

1¼"   ⅝"   ⅝" (16mm)
(3cm)   (16mm)

⅝"
(16mm)   ⅝" (16mm)

LEFT BACK   RIGHT BACK

RIGHT SIDE   RIGHT SIDE

c. Fold the waistband's unattached edge under ⅜" (10mm) on the inside of your skirt so that the fold hangs a bit lower than the existing seam. Pin, then sew the seam allowance with the zipper foot on the right side of your skirt in the "ditch" created by the existing seam, making sure that you catch the fabric on the other side.

4. Sew Your Buttons

Make three evenly spaced buttonholes on the left tab of the waistband and sew three corresponding buttons on the right side. On the front of your waistband, sew six buttons as indicated on the pattern piece.

5. Finish Your Skirt

Hem your skirt with a 1" (2.5cm) hem allowance: fold the bottom-cut edge ½" (13mm), then fold ½" (13mm) again, hiding the raw edge. Press your skirt and do a final thread check.

Back in a Sash

This flirty skirt has a sash inspired by a bow on a package, making it the perfect piece for a holiday party.

Materials List

- ☐ Flare pattern, skirt front only (page 105)
- ☐ Basic sewing supplies
- ☐ 2¼ yds (2m) main fabric
- ☐ Paper
- ☐ Sash template (page 112)
- ☐ 12" (30.5cm) invisible zipper
- ☐ ½ yd (45.5cm) contrast fabric
- ☐ 1 yd (0.9m) 45" (114cm) wide fusible interfacing

FABRIC TIP: We used a solid-colored, cotton twill for the skirt and a printed silk charmeuse for the sash. This is the perfect skirt to play around with pattern and color combinations.

1. Make Your Basic Skirt

This project uses only the Flare skirt-front pattern piece—Back in a Sash doesn't have a center-back seam.

Cut two skirt fronts from your fabric.

2. Make Your Waistband

a. Measure the top of one of your skirt fronts from side edge to side edge; this measurement includes your seam allowance. Call this measurement A.

b. Create a rectangular pattern that is 8¾" (22.5cm) wide by the length of measurement A. (If you don't have paper long enough to accommodate the pattern, tape a few pieces together.) Cut one waistband out of main fabric, one out of contrast fabric, and two out of fusible interfacing. Going forward, we will refer to the main-fabric piece as "waistband front" and the contrast piece as "waistband back."

c. Fuse the interfacing to the wrong sides of the waistband-fabric pieces.

3. Make Your Sash

a. To make your sash pattern, you need a piece of paper that is at least 5" (12.5cm) wide by 39" (99cm) long. Extend the sash pattern 29¼" (74cm) where indicated.

b. Cut out two sash pieces on the fold of both the contrast fabric and interfacing for a total of four sash pieces.

c. Fuse the interfacing to the wrong sides of the two sash-fabric pieces.

d. Fold each sash piece lengthwise, right sides together, and stitch together at a ⅝" (16mm) seam allowance, leaving the short, straight edge open. Trim excess fabric from the tips and clip the curves; then turn right sides out and press.

4. Attach Your Waistband and Sash

a. Before you attach the waistband, decide which skirt piece will be the front and which will be the back—they are identical, so it's up to you. From here on, we will refer to these two pieces as "skirt front" and "skirt back."

b. Fold the skirt front and waistband front in half lengthwise and place a pin in the center of each. With right sides together, pin the waistband front to the skirt front, matching up the center pins and side edges.

> **TIP:** *If your fabric is directional or has a nap to it, make sure it's facing in the same direction before sewing the two pieces together.*

c. Sew the waistband front to the skirt front at a ⅝" (16mm) seam allowance. Repeat with the skirt back and waistband back. Press the seam allowances on both sides up toward the waistband.

d. With the folded edges of the sash pieces positioned up, match the raw edges of the sashes with the raw edges of the waistband on your skirt back. One sash piece will go on the right side and the other will go on the left side. Place the edges of your sash pieces between the seam where the waistband is attached to the skirt and the halfway point of the waistband.

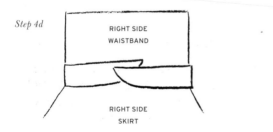

Step 4d

RIGHT SIDE
WAISTBAND

RIGHT SIDE
SKIRT

NOTE: The waistband is double the height of the finished sash pieces, plus ⅝" (16mm) seam allowances on all sides.

e. Baste in place at ⅜" (10mm).

f. Do a pin fit: your waistband should be snug and not gap on your body when worn, so make any necessary adjustments before moving on.

5. Sew Your Invisible Zipper and Side Seams

a. Place the zipper in the left-side seam. Follow Step 3 in Building Your Basic Skirt (page 17), keeping these things in mind:

- The stopper of the zipper will line up with the top of the sash, as the rest of the waistband will be folded toward the inside of the skirt; the seam where the waistband attaches to the skirt should line up on both the back and front pieces.

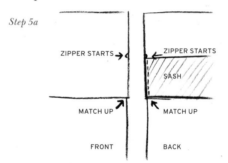

Step 5a

ZIPPER STARTS →⊲ | ⊳← ZIPPER STARTS

SASH

MATCH UP ↗ | ↖ MATCH UP

FRONT | BACK

- Because you're sewing the zipper into a side seam, substitute skirt front for the "left-back piece" and skirt back for "right-back piece."

- The zipper for this skirt is 12" (30.5cm) long rather than 9" (23cm).

b. To sew the right-side seam, lay the front and back pieces right sides together. Pin and sew at a ⅝" (16mm) seam allowance from the top of the waistband to the bottom of the skirt.

NOTE: Pay special attention when sewing the front and back together that you match up waistband seams and that the seam allowance at the waistband goes up toward the waistband.

c. Finish the seam allowance edges separately and press the seam open.

6. Finish Your Waistband

a. Open the zipper and, starting with the back, fold down the portion of the waistband above the sash so that the edges meet up right sides together and the fold is at the top of the sash. Be sure to tuck the top of the zipper tape into the seam.

b. With the zipper foot, stitch the remainder of the waistband to the seam allowance, next to where you have put in your zipper, at slightly less than a $5/8$" (16mm) seam allowance. Stop $5/8$" (16mm) from the bottom of the waistband.

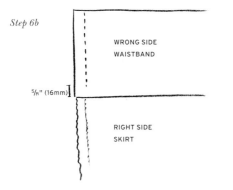

Step 6b

WRONG SIDE
WAISTBAND

$5/8$" (16mm)

RIGHT SIDE
SKIRT

c. Repeat this step for the front, making sure that you fold at the same spot in the waistband—you don't have the sash for reference.

d. Clip excess fabric from your corners, fold right side out, and press. Do a zipper check: when your skirt is zipped up and your sash is tied, the zipper should be hidden.

e. Fold the waistband's unattached edge under $3/8$" (10mm) on the inside of your skirt so that the fold hangs a bit lower than the existing seam. Pin, then sew the seam allowance with the zipper foot on the right side of your skirt in the "ditch" created by the existing seam, making sure that you catch the fabric on the other side.

7. Finish Your Skirt

Hem your skirt with a 1" (2.5cm) hem allowance: fold the bottom-cut edge ½" (13mm), then fold ½" (13mm) again, hiding the raw edge; stitch. Press your skirt and do a final thread check.

FLARE NO.6

Totally Transparent

A lining can really change the look of a skirt, especially when paired with eyelet fabric that allows you to see the lining peeking out behind the shell.

Materials List

- ☐ Flare pattern (pages 105–107)
- ☐ Basic sewing supplies
- ☐ 2¼ yds (2m) outer-shell fabric
- ☐ 2¼ yds (2m) lining fabric
- ☐ 9" (23cm) invisible zipper
- ☐ ¼ yd (23cm) 45" (114cm) wide fusible interfacing
- ☐ Button

FABRIC TIP: We layered a solid-colored eyelet over a striped, lightweight cotton. Have fun mixing and matching your fabrics.

1. Make Your Basic Skirts

Begin making two Flare skirts—the outer shell and the lining—by following Steps 1–2 in Building Your Basic Skirt (page 16) with two exceptions:

- ❦ Cut the lining fabric 1½" (3.8cm) shorter.
- ❦ Cut only one waistband piece out of fusible interfacing.

> **TIP:** *If you are using different-colored fabrics and don't want to keep switching your thread color accordingly, use only the thread that matches the exterior fabric. For our skirt, pink stitches (that match the pink shell) on the hemline of our green-and-white lining is a nice touch and a time-saver!*

2. Finish Your Seam Edges and Sew Your Zipper

a. Finish the center-back seam edges on all four pieces separately.

b. Face the right side of the lining to the wrong side of the outer shell and baste the two skirts together at the first 8" (20cm) of the back seam with a ³⁄₈" (10mm) seam allowance.

c. Follow Steps 3b–f in Building Your Basic Skirt (page 17) to sew the invisible zipper.

3. Finish Your Center-Back Seam

a. Starting with the outer shell, pin and sew the rest of the center-back seam; fold the lining fabric out of the way to expose only the outer-shell fabric. Use the zipper foot to sew a ⁵⁄₈" (16mm) seam allowance from where the stitching for the zipper ends to the bottom of your skirt.

b. On the outer shell only, clip from the edge of the seam allowance to where you started the line of stitching below the zipper. Press this seam allowance open.

c. Move the outer shell out of the way and work with just the lining. Pin the remainder of the center-back seam together. With the zipper foot, sew a ⁵⁄₈" (16mm) seam allowance from below the zipper stitches to the hem. Press the seam allowance open.

Step 3b

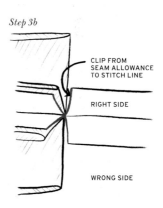

CLIP FROM SEAM ALLOWANCE TO STITCH LINE

RIGHT SIDE

WRONG SIDE

d. Go back to where you clipped your seam allowance (Step 3b) and stitch the area with an over-edge zigzag stitch. Tack down the bottom tab of the zipper to the lining's seam allowance only with a few stitches done with the zipper foot.

4. Pin-Fit Your Skirts

Match up your skirt fronts and backs, right sides together. Place safety pins every 3" (7.5cm) along the side seams at a ⅝" (16mm) seam allowance.

5. Sew Your Side Seams

Sew both sets of side seams separately. If you did not make any changes when pin-fitting, stitch the side seams at a ⅝" (16mm) seam allowance; if you adjusted the safety pins, chalk a vertical mark over each pin, then connect your vertical marks into a continuous line on both sides of your skirts. Sew along these new stitching lines, then trim the seam allowances to ⅝" (16mm). Finish the seam allowances.

6. Sew Your Waistband

a. Sew around the entire top edge, joining your layers into one skirt.

NOTE: Sew over your original stay-stitching.

b. Convert the three waistband pieces (outer shell, lining, and interfacing) into one piece: Fuse the interfacing to the wrong side of the lining piece. Face the wrong side of the outer-shell piece to the right side of the lining. Pin around the edges and baste ⅜" (10mm) from the edges.

c. With the edge of the waistband even with the top-cut edge of the skirt, right sides together, overlap your waistband ⅝" (16mm) past the right zipper edge. Pin both layers together until you reach the other side of the zipper. Sew a ⅝" (16mm) seam allowance all the way around the top of your skirt,

starting and stopping at the zipper. Trim the left edge of the waistband down to 1⅞" (4.5cm), if necessary.

d. Fold your waistband in half, right sides together. On the right-back side, sew the edge of the waistband at a ⅝" (16mm) seam allowance, stopping ⅝" (16mm) from the bottom corner. On the left-back side, sew the edge at a ⅝" (16mm) seam allowance, pivot ⅝" (16mm) from the bottom corner, then continue sewing 1¼" (3cm). Clip the corners and press the seam allowance up toward the waistband. Turn the waistband right side out and poke out the corners of the tabs.

e. Fold the waistband's unattached edge under ⅜" (10mm) on the inside of your skirt so that the fold hangs a bit lower than the existing seam. Pin, then sew the seam allowance with the zipper foot on the right side of your skirt in the "ditch" created by the existing seam, making sure that you catch the fabric on the other side.

f. Press the waistband, then make a buttonhole—one that corresponds to the size of your button—in the left-side tab. Sew your button onto the right side of the waistband.

7. Finish Your Skirt

Hem your outer-shell and lining separately with a 1" (2.5cm) hem allowance: Fold the bottom-cut edges 1/2" (13mm), then fold 1/2" (13mm) again, hiding the raw edges; stitch. Press your skirt and do a final thread check.

Patterns & Templates

A-line Skirt: Front

ENLARGE 400% OR DRAFT
(the distance between each dot equals 1", or 2.5cm)

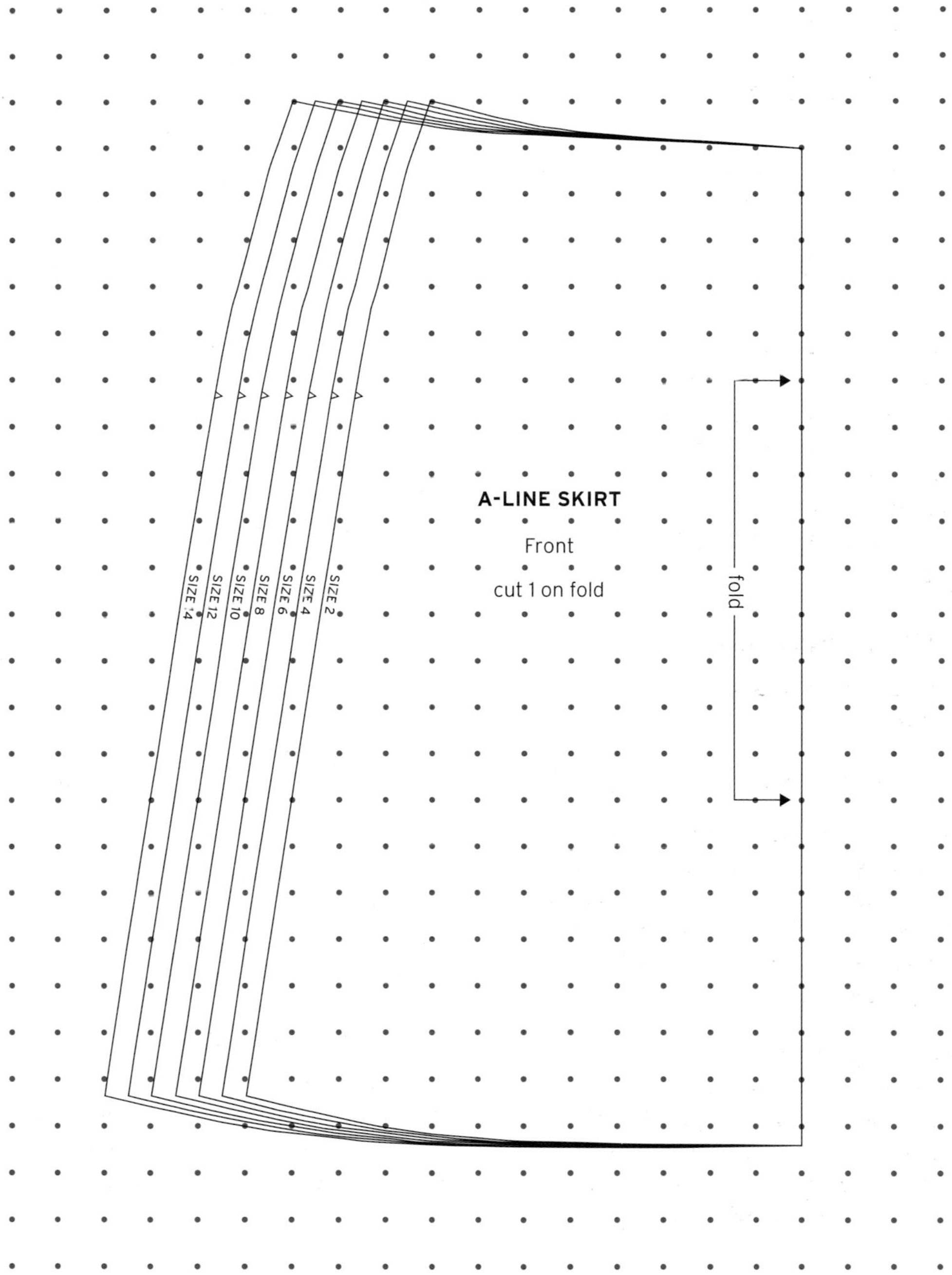

A-LINE SKIRT

Front

cut 1 on fold

fold

SIZE 14 SIZE 12 SIZE 10 SIZE 8 SIZE 6 SIZE 4 SIZE 2

A-line Skirt: Back

ENLARGE 400% OR DRAFT
(the distance between each dot equals 1", or 2.5cm)

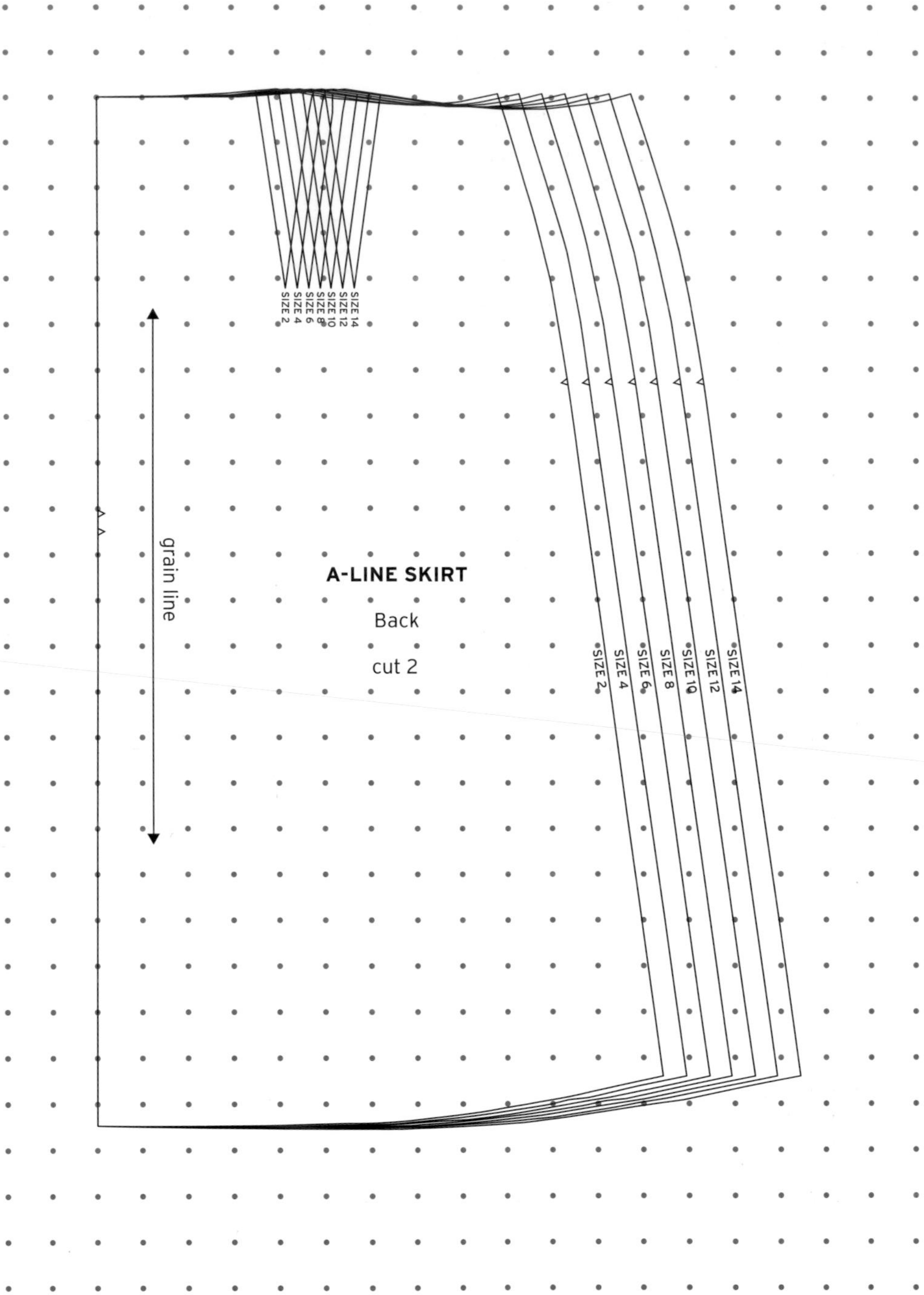

grain line

SIZE 14
SIZE 12
SIZE 10
SIZE 8
SIZE 6
SIZE 4
SIZE 2

A-LINE SKIRT

Back

cut 2

SIZE 2
SIZE 4
SIZE 6
SIZE 8
SIZE 10
SIZE 12
SIZE 14

Pencil Skirt: Front

ENLARGE 400% OR DRAFT
(the distance between each dot equals 1", or 2.5cm)

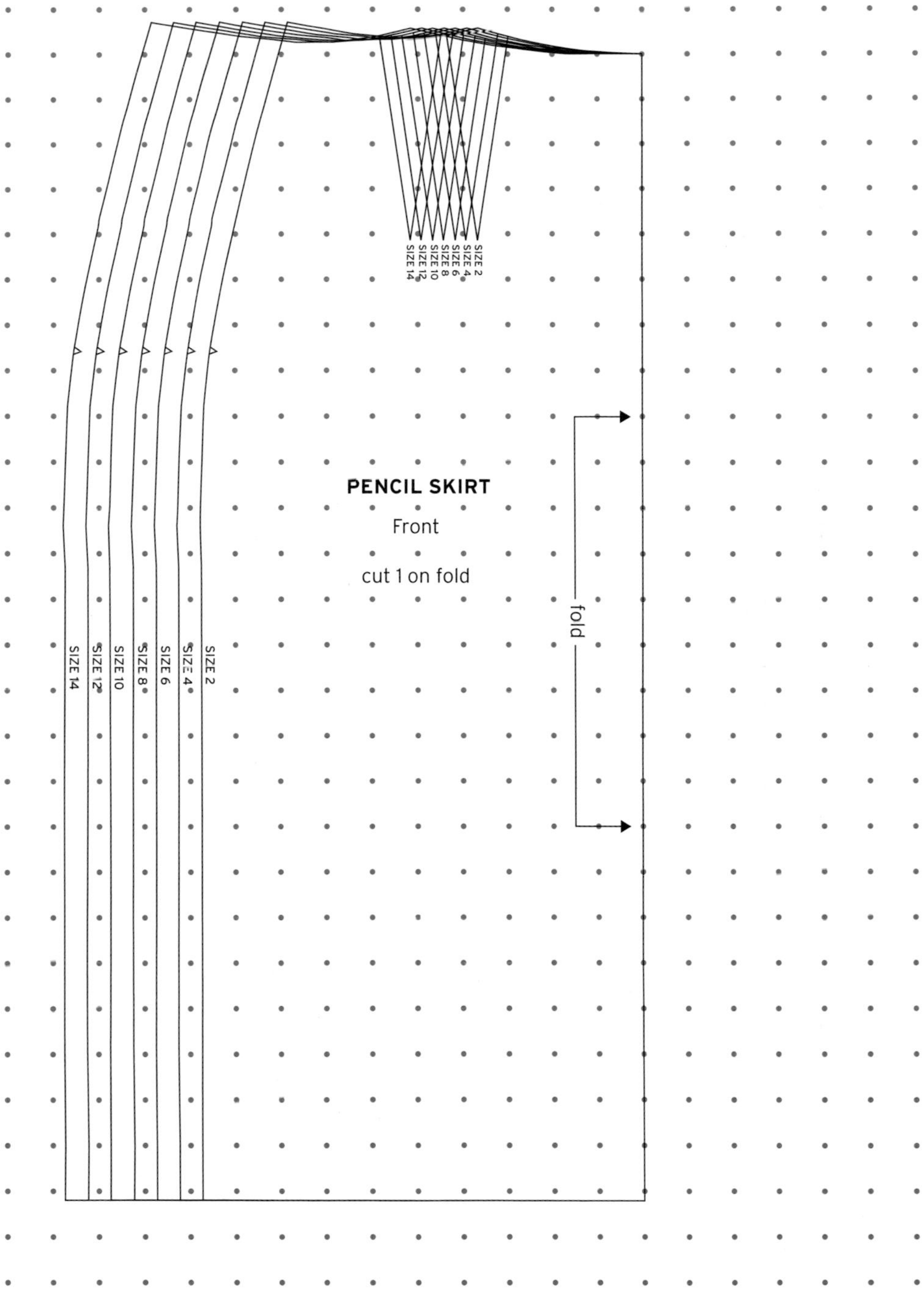

SIZE 2
SIZE 4
SIZE 6
SIZE 8
SIZE 10
SIZE 12
SIZE 14

PENCIL SKIRT

Front

cut 1 on fold

fold

SIZE 14
SIZE 12
SIZE 10
SIZE 8
SIZE 6
SIZE 4
SIZE 2

Pencil Skirt: Back

ENLARGE 400% OR DRAFT
(the distance between each dot equals 1", or 2.5cm)

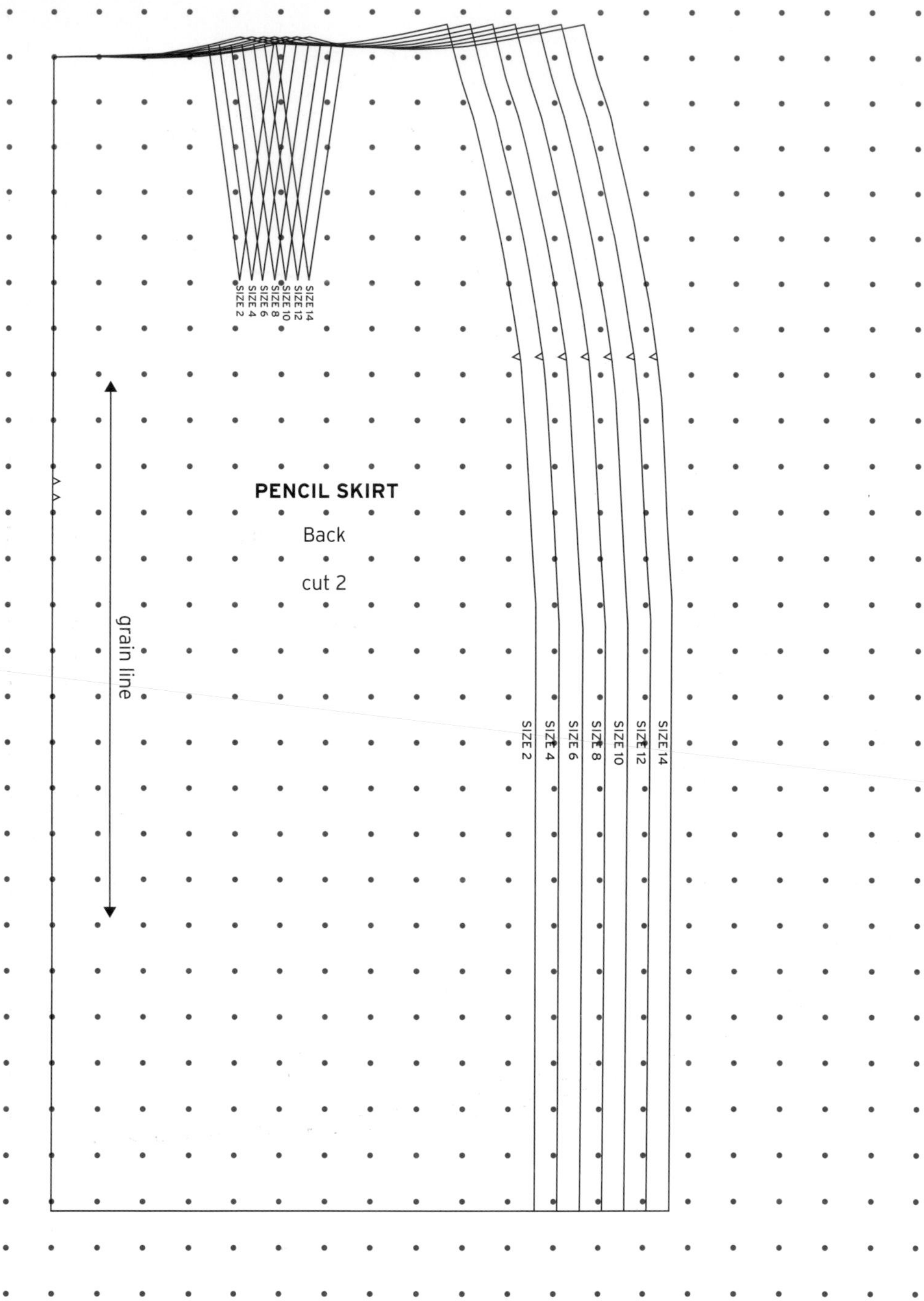

SIZE 14
SIZE 12
SIZE 10
SIZE 8
SIZE 6
SIZE 4
SIZE 2

PENCIL SKIRT

Back

cut 2

grain line

SIZE 2
SIZE 4
SIZE 6
SIZE 8
SIZE 10
SIZE 12
SIZE 14

Flare Skirt: Front

ENLARGE 400% OR DRAFT
(the distance between each dot equals 1", or 2.5cm)

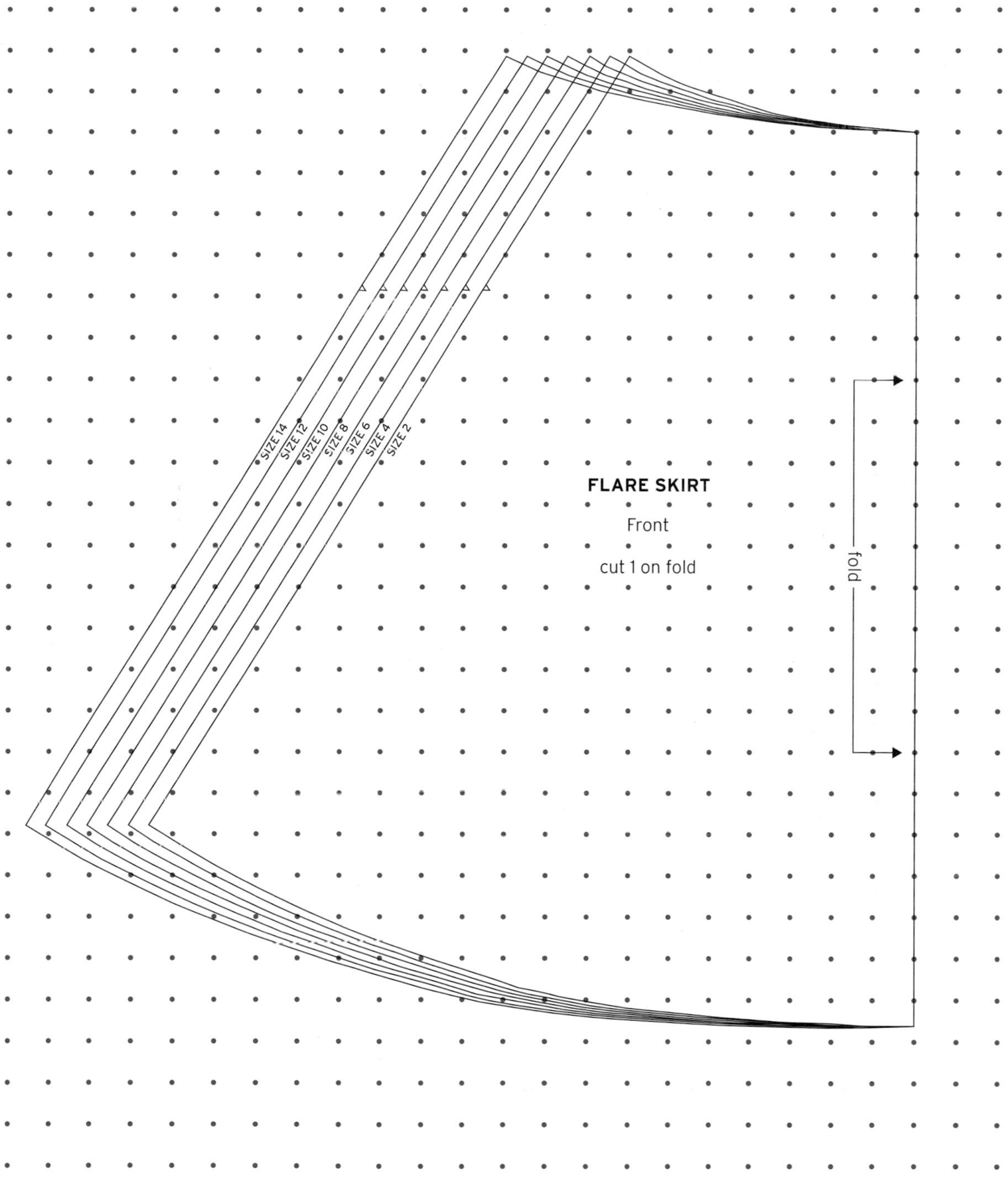

SIZE 14 SIZE 12 SIZE 10 SIZE 8 SIZE 6 SIZE 4 SIZE 2

FLARE SKIRT

Front

cut 1 on fold

fold

Flare Skirt: Back

ENLARGE 400% OR DRAFT
(the distance between each dot equals 1", or 2.5cm)

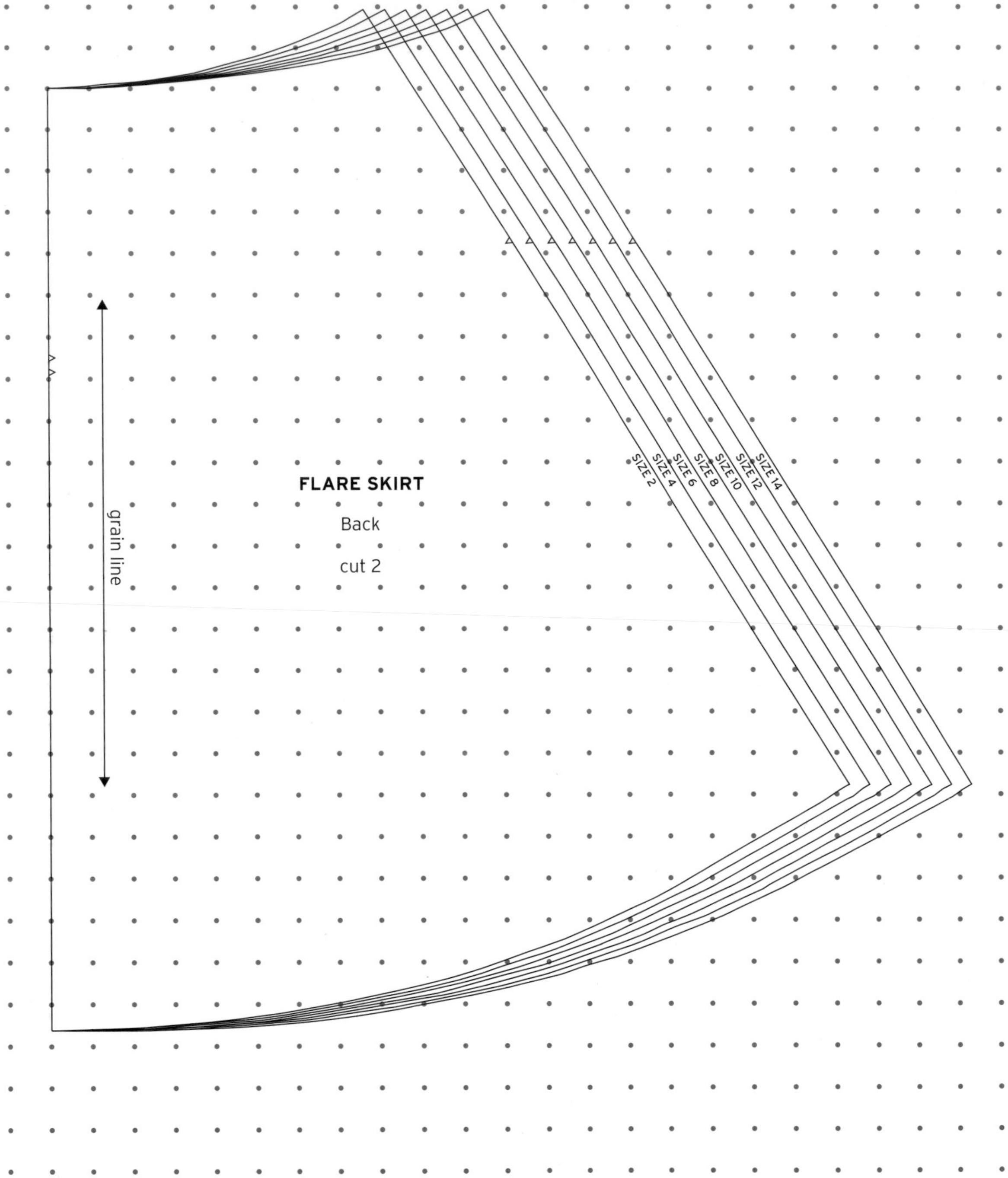

grain line

FLARE SKIRT

Back

cut 2

SIZE 2 SIZE 4 SIZE 6 SIZE 8 SIZE 10 SIZE 12 SIZE 14

Flare Skirt: Waistband

ENLARGE 400% OR DRAFT
(the distance between each dot equals 1", or 2.5cm)

SIZE 14 · SIZE 12 · SIZE 10 · SIZE 8 · SIZE 6 · SIZE 4 · SIZE 2

FLARE SKIRT

Waistband

cut 1 on fold of fabric / cut 1 on fold of interfacing

fold

Kind of Sketchy: Image 1

ENLARGE 200% OR DRAFT
(the distance between each dot equals 1", or 2.5cm)

align circles and connect to Image 2

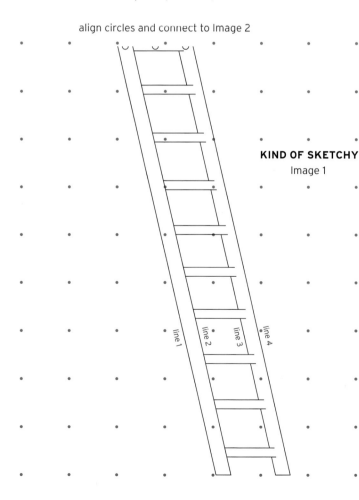

KIND OF SKETCHY

Image 1

line 1 · line 2 · line 3 · line 4

Kind of Sketchy: Image 2

ENLARGE 200% OR DRAFT
(the distance between each dot equals 1", or 2.5cm)

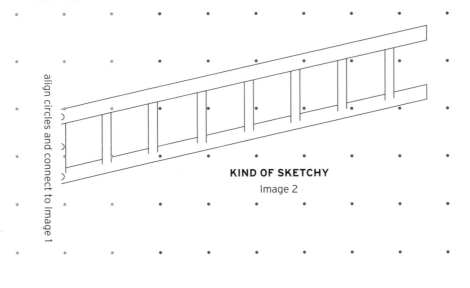

align circles and connect to Image 1

KIND OF SKETCHY
Image 2

Kind of Sketchy: Image 3

ENLARGE 200% OR DRAFT
(the distance between each dot equals 1", or 2.5cm)

KIND OF SKETCHY
Image 3

Cute as a Button: Scallop

ENLARGE 200% OR DRAFT
(the distance between each dot equals 1", or 2.5cm)

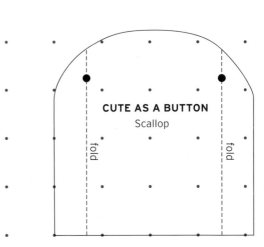

CUTE AS A BUTTON
Scallop

fold

fold

Put It in Print: Stencil

ENLARGE 133% OR DRAFT
(the distance between each dot equals 1", or 2.5cm)

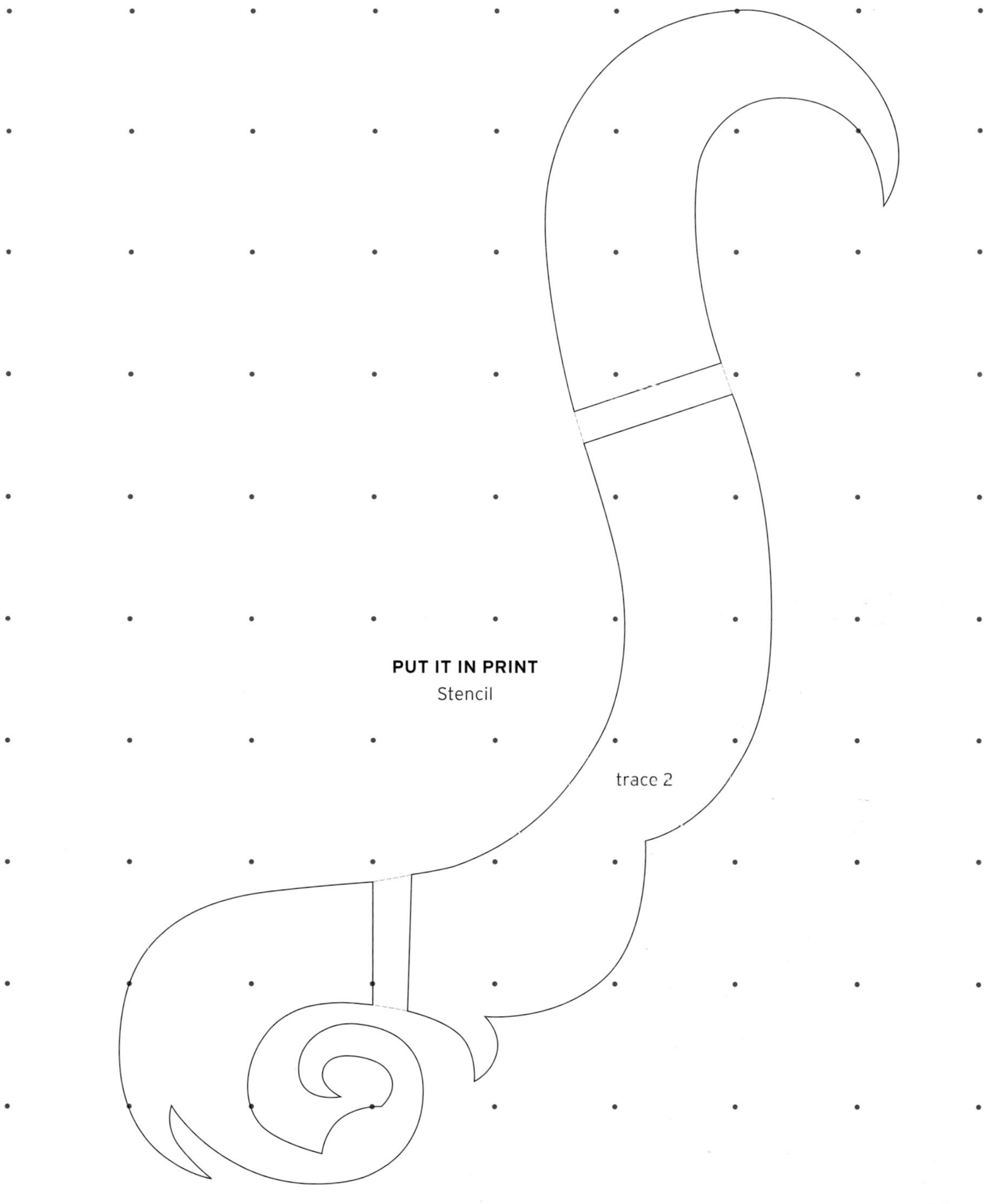

PUT IT IN PRINT
Stencil

trace 2

Rosie the Riveter: Apron 1

ENLARGE 200% OR DRAFT
(the distance between each dot equals 1", or 2.5cm)

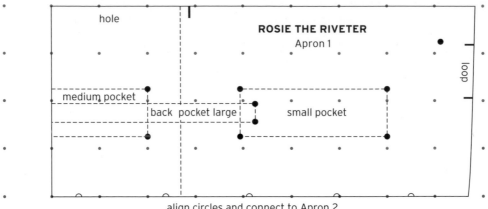

align circles and connect to Apron 2

Rosie the Riveter: Apron 2

ENLARGE 200% OR DRAFT
(the distance between each dot equals 1", or 2.5cm)

align circles and connect to Apron 1

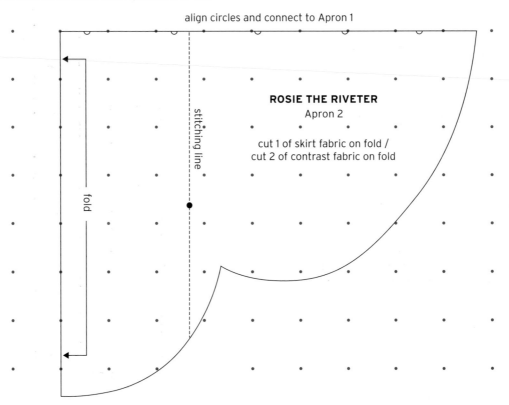

Don't Hem Me In: Sculpted Hem 1

Rosie the Riveter: Hardware Loop

ENLARGE 133% OR DRAFT
(the distance between each dot equals 1", or 2.5cm)

Large Pocket Facing

ENLARGE 133% OR DRAFT (the distance between each dot equals 1", or 2.5cm)

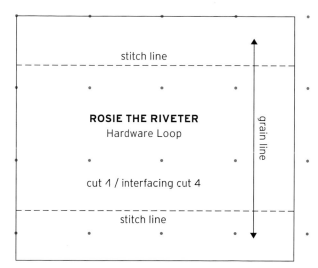

stitch line

ROSIE THE RIVETER
Hardware Loop

cut 1 / interfacing cut 4

stitch line

grain line

grain line

ROSIE THE RIVETER
Large Pocket Facing

cut 1 / interfacing cut 1

Rosie the Riveter: Small Pocket Facing

ENLARGE 133% OR DRAFT
(the distance between each dot equals 1", or 2.5cm)

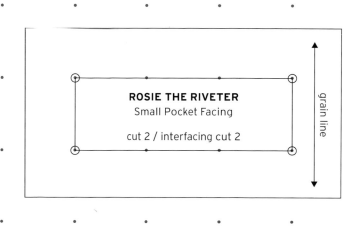

ROSIE THE RIVETER
Small Pocket Facing

cut 2 / interfacing cut 2

grain line

Putting Your Look Together

After a decade of owning and operating clothing boutiques, we've realized that falling in love with a fantastic skirt on the hanger is only half the battle. To look great in it, you've got to know what to wear *with* it. Here, we've outlined a few basic guidelines to follow when it comes to pairing your skirt with the rest of your outfit. These are not, by any means, strict; as a matter of fact, we believe you should get as creative as possible and express yourself. But through experience, we also know that some people prefer having a little guidance.

Tops

A-LINE

This skirt is the easiest style to pair with tops because it's equally chic dressed up or down. For a casual daytime look, wear a comfy, scoop-necked tee that hits around your hips. For a more pulled-together look, try a tailored button-down—untucked with the first couple of buttons open—topped with a knit vest.

PENCIL

Pair this skirt with tops that highlight your waist and showcase the Pencil's slim line. Fitted tees, tailored button-downs, tops with a peplum, and snug vests look great with this shape. If you want a more casual look, try a looser-fitting shirt under a fitted blazer.

FLARE

Because it has so much volume, this skirt calls for a fitted top. Try a cowl-necked knit or a clingy tee.

LAYERING

When layering on top, try to have one fitted piece—
a vest, blazer, or sweater. Too many loose layers can
create extra bulk.

TUCKING IN

Make sure you have a bit of drape to your tucked-in
top. Some people can tuck in a very fitted tank
and look great, but most of us need a little drape
to flatter the waist area. Try tucking in tops made
of fabrics like silk or rayon, which have a good
amount of natural drape. When "blousing," you
don't want too much fabric to hang over your
skirt—just enough to emphasize the waist. Also,
using a belt to delineate the waist always looks
good; just make sure it doesn't obstruct any detail
on the skirt. The Flare skirt looks especially great
belted at the waistline.

Pattern & Color

PATTERN

If your skirt is busy, the rest of your outfit should
remain simple. We used a bold fabric for Summer
in the City (page 84), so we paired it with a solid-
colored top that coordinates with one of the colors
in the skirt's print. For shoes, we went with simple
black flats, to keep the emphasis on the skirt.

COLOR

If you match your top to a color in your skirt, take
your shoes in a different direction. The last thing
you want are turquoise shoes paired with a turquoise shirt; it's too matchy-matchy. If your top is
a bright solid and your skirt is patterned, choose a
neutral sandal, a brown boot, or a metallic heel.

Accessories

There is definitely such a thing as over-accessoriz-
ing. If you are wearing earrings, forgo the necklace
and instead throw on a couple of bangles or a hat.
If your outfit is extremely colorful, try one large
cocktail ring and leave it at that. Mixing too many
elements can overwhelm your look, so always take
one away, just in case.

Cold-Weather Dressing

We have noticed that during the wintertime, people
tend to shy away from bright colors and slip into
the doldrums of black, brown, and gray. Your
wardrobe doesn't have to match the sky outside.
Try wearing a white or floral-patterned skirt with
black tights, boots, and a woolly cardigan. Doing
so will not only increase your wardrobe choices, it
will also extend the seasonality of many garments—
not to mention bring a little warmth to an otherwise
chilly day.

Glossary

Basting stitch: Using a sewing machine's longest straight stitch, this stitching technique joins fabrics temporarily.

Bias: The 45-degree angle of fabric; woven fabrics stretch along the bias line.

Bias tape: Long strips of fabric cut on the bias that are used for a number of functions, including finishing seam edges and hems.

Blind hem: A hemming technique where the stitches are practically invisible from the outside of the garment. Most machines have this stitch option and come with a blind-hem foot.

Box pleat: Two single pleats that butt up against each other yet face in the opposite direction.

Clipping corners: Removing extra fabric from the corner of a seam allowance to alleviate bulk when turned right side out.

Clipping curves: Cutting into the seam allowance of a curved seam to allow the seam allowance to bend. For an inside curve, cut a V in the seam allowance to reduce bulk; for an outside curve cut straight in toward the stitches to open the seam allowance.

Cross-grain: Fabric threads that run perpendicular to the selvage; this is also known as weft.

Dart: A sewing device that gives shape to a garment; it is illustrated on a pattern as a triangle or a diamond.

Dart legs: The lines of the dart that extend out from the dart tip. When matched up with each other, they act as the stitching line to sew the dart.

Dart tip: The bottom of the dart that is a point; a dart is sewn from the top of the dart legs to the dart tip.

Ease: The number of inches added to a garment's measurements to allow for comfort of movement.

Easing: The fitting together of different-sized fabric pieces using a gathering stitch.

French seam: A neatly finished seam in which the raw edges on fabrics are tucked and sewn in to prevent fraying and unraveling.

Fold: The edge created by doubling fabric.

Fold line: The symbol on a pattern that indicates that the pattern piece should be placed on the fold, resulting in a fabric piece that is one piece when unfolded.

Gathering stitch: A stitching technique that uses a sewing machine's longest straight stitch, leaving threads hanging on either end; while holding one of the threads, the fabric is slid over the thread to help with easing.

Grain line: Fabric threads that run parallel to the selvage; this is also known as warp. When a pattern has a grain-line symbol, the line on the pattern needs to be parallel to the fabric's selvage edge.

Hemline: The line on a pattern or piece of fabric that will be the finished hem.

Invisible zipper foot: A removable presser foot for a sewing machine designed to push the coils of a invisible zipper to the side while stitching right next to them.

Lockstitching: Stitching forward and backward with a sewing machine over the same set of stitches to keep them from unraveling.

Nap/Direction: Fabric like corduroy and velvet has nap, or texture, that needs to be cut in a certain direction. Patterned fabric may also need to be cut in a specific direction.

Notches: Triangular markings on a pattern piece that, when transferred to the fabric, aid in matching up pattern pieces correctly.

Over-edge zigzag stitch: Using a sewing machine's zigzag stitch at a middle length and width to sew over the edge of a fabric to finish the fabric's raw edge and keep it from fraying.

Pivot: Changing direction in a line of stitching by leaving your needle in the fabric, lifting your presser foot, turning your fabric according to the pattern, putting the presser foot down, and sewing again.

Pleat: A type of fold created by folding fabric back on itself and stitching it in place.

Pressing: The act of using the heat of an iron to get the fibers of your fabric to lie in a particular direction.

Right side: The side of a fabric that will be visible on a finished project.

Seam allowance: The amount of space from the cut edge to where your stitches are sewn into your fabric. Our seam allowance is ⅝" (16mm) unless otherwise specified.

Selvage: The straight, finished edge created when a fabric is woven on the loom. Fabric width is measured from one selvage edge to the other.

Snipping: Making a small cut in fabric within the seam allowance as a marking indicator.

Stay-stitching: A straight stitch sewn closely to the fabric edge to keep fabric from fraying and to prevent curves from stretching out.

Stitch length: The distance between stitches on a sewing machine. Every sewing machine has a variety of stitch lengths—the longest is typically used for gathering and basting; the middle length, for general sewing of seams; and the shortest, for reinforcing specific areas.

Stretch stitch: A very strong sewing-machine stitch that goes forward, backward, and forward again; the symbol for it on a machine is a group of vertical, perforated lines.

Symbols/markings: Information, like darts, on pattern pieces that is indicated by lines, triangles, or other shapes and that must be transferred to fabric.

Topstitching: A stitching technique done on the right side of the fabric that keeps seam allowances in place; it is also used decoratively.

Wrong side: The side of a fabric that is unseen on a finished garment.

Zipper foot: An attachment to the sewing machine designed to sew closely to the coils of a zipper while putting even pressure on all layers of fabric; it is also used for attaching trim that has a thicker decorative edge.

Zipper pull: The part of the zipper that when pulled on allows you to open or close the zipper.

Resources

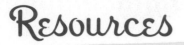

SEWING SUPPLIES AND NOTIONS

Jo-Ann Fabric and Craft Stores
joann.com

P&S Fabrics
(212) 226-1534

Sil Thread
threadus.com

FABRIC

B&J Fabrics
bandjfabrics.com

Chic Fabrics
(212) 398-9451

Metro Textiles
metrotextile.blogspot.com

New York Elegant Fabrics
nyelegantfabrics.com

Repro Depot Fabrics
reprodepot.com

Rosen & Chadick Fabrics
rosenandchadickfabrics.com

Somewhere In Time
(vintage fabrics)
(732) 247-3636

Spandex House
spandexhouse.com

TRIM

Daytona Trimming
daytonatrim.com

Fiber Notion
fibernotion.com

M&J Trimming
mjtrim.com

Pacific Trimming
pacifictrimming.com

FABRIC PAINT

Blick Art Materials
dickblick.com

Dharma Trading
dharmatrading.com

CLOTHING AND ACCESSORIES

Agapantha
agapanthanyc.bigcartel.com

Alternative Apparel
alternativeapparel.com

Astridland
astridland.com

Cinderloop
cinderloop.com

Farylrobin
farylrobin.com

Flirt Brooklyn
flirt-brooklyn.com

Jeffrey Campbell
jeffreycampbellshoes.com

Melissa Bell
melissabellnyc.blogspot.com

Reverie
reverienyc.com

Samoy Lenko
samoylenko.com

Zachary Pryor
zp-nyc.com

FAVORITE WEBSITES

Built By Wendy
builtbywendy.com

Cal Patch's Hodge Podge Farm
hodgepodgefarm.net

Full Swing Textiles
fullswingtextiles.com

Lotta Jansdotter
jansdotter.com

Smart Flix
smartflix.com

Westminster Fibers
westminsterfibers.com

Index

Acknowledgments

First and foremost, we want to thank Heather Falcone, the original Flirt girl: It is your vision that set the wheels in motion. Your ability to make everything you touch look beautiful brought Flirt to the attention of Brooklyn, by making everyone who walked by want to come into our shop. Without you, Flirt would not be, and neither would this book!

To Emily Gcanacopoulos—manager, saleswoman, seamstress, and overall superhero: Thank you for picking up the slack at Flirt while we wrote this book.

To our beautiful models—Emily Geanacopoulos, Dawn Giambalvo, Linda Holm, Liv Lee, Johanna Neufeld, Dani Paquin, Lindy Parker, Nicole Provonsil, Brielle Silvestri: You are all positively beautiful, and we are so happy that you were willing to represent Flirt and make our designs come to life!

To Flirt girls past and present: Thank you for being that first impression that brings people back to Flirt over and over again.

To our loyal Flirt customers and our students at Home Ec: Thank you for believing in what we do as much as we do, and helping us realize so many of our dreams by keeping us in business for all of these years.

To Avril Griswold, Bob and Dorothy Gilstrap, Brad Bates, Steve Cherny, and the rest of our family and friends: Thank you for supporting us while we pursued our goals and not discouraging us from thinking big.

To all the creative independent designers who have helped stock the racks and shelves of Flirt over the years: You helped us become the unique place we are by being the unique people you are.

To Alisa Blanter: Thank you for creating our beautiful website, which became the inspiration for the design of this book.

To Sharyn Rosart, Lynne Yeamans, Erin Canning, and the rest of the team at Quirk Packaging: Thank you for seeing something special in what we do and wanting to turn it into a book.

To Barbara Sullivan: Thank you for the beautiful photos that captured exactly the look we wanted. We couldn't have been happier with how they turned out.

To Lana Lê: Thank you for the beautiful book design and fabulous illustrations, which help our words make much more sense than they would otherwise.

To Betty Wong and the rest of the team at Potter Craft: Thank you for giving us this fantastic opportunity to share what we do with such a huge audience.

To Henson: Thank you for keeping us company and tolerating many late nights and many missed walks. You are missed.

About the Authors

Flirt Brooklyn, Inc., was established in June 2000, by Patti Gilstrap, Seryn Potter, and Heather Falcone, in a small storefront on a somewhat uninhabited street in Brooklyn, New York. The store was one of a few pioneers on Smith Street, which now, ten years later, is teeming with trendy boutiques, restaurants, and other specialty shops. In 2004, Flirt expanded its reach into Brooklyn with a much larger shop on Park Slope's busy Fifth Avenue; in 2007, Patti and Seryn realized one of their dreams by opening a large sewing studio called Home Ec, where they design and manufacture clothing and teach beginner and intermediate sewing classes. In 2010, they crossed the bridge into Manhattan to become co-owners of the Union Square boutique Apartment 141.

The Flirt boutiques feature a namesake line of clothing and a custom-skirt service, which allows customers to choose styles and fabrics, creating one-of-a-kind skirts. Along with clothing and accessories by many other designers from New York City and beyond, Flirt has created a venue for independent designers to showcase what they do. Flirt is Zagat-rated and was voted Citysearch's Best Brooklyn Boutique in 2007. Patterns by Flirt Brooklyn are available through the McCall Pattern Company. Visit Flirt at www.flirt-brooklyn.com.

Patti Gilstrap *(right)* came to New York City to pursue dance, choreography, and design. After touring as a wardrobe supervisor with Alvin Ailey, she spent a number of years touring the United States and abroad as a puppeteer with the NYC-based Hudson Vagabond Puppets. At the same time, she choreographed a number of well-received modern dance pieces of her own, while also costuming many well-known NYC-based modern dance companies.

Seryn Potter *(left)* landed in New York City, intent on pursuing a career in music. She spent time as a singer and guitar player in a number of bands, and found herself playing on some of the best small stages in NYC. She made two albums before turning her attention to Flirt, and now does most of her singing to her daughter, Ellie Bell.